Researching Student Learning in Higher Education

Many contemporary concerns in higher education focus on the student experience of learning. With a larger and much more diverse intake than ever before, linked with a declining unit of resource, questions are being asked afresh around the purposes of higher education. Although much of the debate is currently focused on issues of student access and success, a simple input–output model of higher education is insufficient.

This book turns this conversation on its head, by inserting a full consideration of student agency into the context of higher education. Working sociologically, it explores the influence of the social context on what the individual student achieves. The theoretical tenets of a social realist approach are laid out in detail in the book; the potential value of this approach is then illustrated by a case study of student learning in engineering education. Employing Margaret Archer's social realist theory, an analysis of student narratives is used to work towards a realist understanding of the underlying mechanisms that constrain and enable student success. Building on this analysis, the book develops a novel set of proposals for potential ways forward in improving student learning in higher education.

Jennifer M. Case is a professor, with a particular focus on academic development, in the Department of Chemical Engineering at the University of Cape Town, South Africa.

The Society for Research into Higher Education (SRHE) is an independent and financially self-supporting international learned Society. It is concerned to advance understanding of higher education, especially through the insights, perspectives and knowledge offered by systematic research and scholarship.

The Society's primary role is to improve the quality of higher education through facilitating knowledge exchange, discourse and publication of research. SRHE members are worldwide and the Society is an NGO in operational relations with UNESCO.

The Society has a wide set of aims and objectives. Amongst its many activities the Society:

• is a specialist publisher of higher education research, journals and books, amongst them Studies in Higher Education, Higher Education Quarterly, Research into Higher Education Abstracts and a long running monograph book series.

The Society also publishes a number of in-house guides and produces a specialist series "Issues in Postgraduate Education".

• funds and supports a large number of special interest networks for researchers and practitioners working in higher education from every discipline. These networks are open to all and offer a range of topical seminars, workshops and other events throughout the year ensuring the Society is in touch with all current research knowledge.

• runs the largest annual UK-based higher education research conference and parallel conference for postgraduate and newer researchers. This is attended by researchers from over 35 countries and showcases current research across every aspect of higher education.

SRHE

Society for Research into Higher Education
Advancing knowledge Informing policy Enhancing practice

73 Collier Street
London N1 9BE
United Kingdom

T +44 (0)20 7427 2350
F +44 (0)20 7278 1135
E srheoffice@srhe.ac.uk

www.srhe.ac.uk

Director: Helen Perkins
Registered Charity No.313850
Company No.00868820
Limited by Guarantee
Registered office as above

Society for Research into Higher Education (SRHE) series

Series Editors: Lynn McAlpine, Oxford Learning Institute
                Jeroen Huisman, University of Bath

Published titles:

Forthcoming titles:

Researching Student Learning in Higher Education

A social realist approach

Jennifer M. Case

Routledge
Taylor & Francis Group

LONDON AND NEW YORK

First published 2013
by Routledge
2 Park Square, Milton Park, Abingdon, Oxon OX14 4RN
together with the Society for Research into Higher Education (SRHE)
73 Collier Street
London N1 9BE
UK

Simultaneously published in the USA and Canada
by Routledge
711 Third Avenue, New York, NY 10017 together with the
Society for Research into Higher Education (SRHE)
73 Collier Street
London N1 9BE
UK

Routledge is an imprint of the Taylor & Francis Group, an informa business

British Library Cataloguing in Publication Data
A catalogue record for this book is available from the British Library

Library of Congress Cataloging in Publication Data
    Case, Jennifer M.
    Researching student learning in higher education :
    a social realist approach / Jennifer M. Case.
    pages cm.—(Research into higher education)
    1. Engineering—Study and teaching (Higher)—South Africa—
    Case studies. 2. College students—Social conditions—
    South Africa—Case studies. 3. Academic achievement—
    Social aspects—South Africa—Case studies. I. Title.
    T166.S7C37 2014
    620.007110968—dc23
    2013005816

ISBN: 978–0–415–66234–5 (hbk)
ISBN: 978–0–415–66235–2 (pbk)
ISBN: 978–0–203–79740–2 (ebk)

Typeset in Galliard
by Swales & Willis Ltd, Exeter, Devon

Printed and bound in Great Britain by
TJ International Ltd, Padstow, Cornwall

Contents

Illustrations

Figures

Tables

Series editors' introduction

This series, co-published by the Society for Research into Higher Education and Routledge Books, aims to provide, in an accessible manner, cutting-edge scholarly thinking and inquiry that reflects the rapidly changing world of higher education, examined in a global context.

Encompassing topics of wide international relevance, the series includes every aspect of the international higher education research agenda, from strategic policy formulation and impact to pragmatic advice on best practice in the field. Each book in the series aims to meet at least one of the principal aims of the Society: to advance knowledge; to enhance practice; to inform policy.

In this volume, Jenni Case analyses student learning in the broad sense. Building on the work of, for instance, Bernstein and Archer, she takes a critical realist stance and argues for research on student learning against a theoretical background stressing structure, culture and agency. The empirical part of the book takes us into a particular case at the University of Cape Town, South Africa and gives us in-depth insight into the learning journeys of engineering students from which to draw pedagogical implications. Living up to the critical realist stance, the possibilities for progressive change are discussed in the last part of the book.

Lynn McAlpine
Jeroen Huisman

Acknowledgements

Students are at the heart of this book, and it is to them that I owe the greatest gratitude. In the larger sense, I have been privileged to work over the years with many cohorts of University of Cape Town (UCT) chemical engineering students, but for this book my particular thanks are reserved for the third-year class of about a decade ago who welcomed me in to their midst as a rather bizarre interloper – a lecturer and education researcher taking time out to get some sense of what it is to be an engineering student. It has been a great pleasure to track down and connect again with the 14 students represented in the case study in this book and to see the extraordinary ways in which they have developed and conducted their life projects so far.

This work has taken shape within an amazingly supportive community of colleagues both at UCT and further abroad. There are too many to name whose interactions have spurred on my thinking and have provided good challenge at key points. Many provided comment and encouragement on very early drafts of part of this work. However, I particularly need to single out the contributions of Delia Marshall from the University of the Western Cape and Kevin Williams from UCT who meticulously read through the full manuscript and provided thoughtful and informed final suggestions. My mother, Glynne Case, has once again done her eagle-eyed proofreading for which I am very grateful. All errors which remain are, of course, for my own account.

The writing of this book would not have been possible without a five-month sabbatical, which was generously supported by the award of a Mandela Fellowship at the W.E.B. Du Bois Institute for African and African American Research at Harvard University. The rich scholarly environment provided there was a great nurturing space, and I am thankful for the tremendous welcome and support that they gave me. I also wish to recognise the financial support of the National Research Foundation of South Africa, which has supported my research over a number of years.

This book is dedicated to my close family and friends, specifically to my parents and to my husband Roger, who, in turn, have supported my academic project including many 'extra projects'. It is also devoted to the memory of my late brother Jimmy, whose own project was tragically cut short. And finally, in the writing of this book I look to the future, celebrating my own children James and Julia, who enrich me in so many ways and who still have ahead of them the interesting challenge of crafting their own life projects.

Introduction

Sizwe[1] is a third-year chemical engineering student at the University of Cape Town (UCT). He comes from a township outside Durban and was brought up by his grandmother along with his cousins; his mother worked as a domestic worker in Johannesburg. When he was in his eighth grade of school his mother became ill and died, and in the following year his grandmother died. These devastating circumstances produced what he describes as a turning point in his life:

> . . . instead of sinking into the facts that actually I'm really an orphan or something like that, something came into my mind that nobody is going to take care of me now, so you better do something, and that's when I started taking my courses seriously at school.

Up to this point Sizwe had been hanging around with township gangsters and had been involved in some minor housebreaking; in an extraordinary way he then started to take charge of his life in order to chart a different future. He managed to obtain scholarships to support his studies and through these funds supported the household of children of which he had become the *de facto* head. The rest was, as they say, history: he went on to study chemical engineering, widely regarded as a tough degree, at one of the country's most prestigious universities. I caught up with him when he was a third-year student while I was undertaking research into student learning in engineering, in the context of the challenges of the post-apartheid social and educational landscape. His story grabbed me with force – a paradigm of the kind of success that we wished for all our students and yet so few achieved. And it was hard to imagine a background that could be tougher than his. How did he do it? From this opening vignette it is clear that here we have an example of an academically talented young man with an extraordinary ability to take his destiny in his own hands, and to turn difficulty into opportunity. The details of Sizwe's story challenged many of my preconceptions around higher education and have provided the departure point for the journey of exploration that is the subject of this book.

While at secondary school Sizwe had read a magazine article about a black chemical engineer working at a paper mill who had come up with an engineering innovation that had saved the company millions of rands. He thought to himself that this sounded like something he would like to do, and he was struck that the person doing it was from a township just like him. In reflecting on the transition into first-year university, contrary to what one might expect, Sizwe found it surprisingly unstressful: for the first time ever in his life he was able to focus just on himself and his books (although he did send a portion of his bursary money home). He revelled in the experience of meeting new people from a range of different backgrounds. He also noted that because at school he had had the experience of failing tests and then working hard to succeed, he was not too bothered by the experience of failing a test at university.

The high workload in the chemical engineering curriculum is well-known, and in interviews most of the other students in Sizwe's class characterised the experience as a form of alienation in which they gave up much of their broader engagement with family, friends and university life, in order to grind their way through the academic demands that faced them. Sizwe's story stood apart in this regard. He was adamant that he needed to maintain a broader connection both to the university and also to his own personal goals for development, and in this way he managed to effect a remarkable balance. As a class representative he felt a responsibility for what he was seeing happening to his classmates, and he jokingly recounted going to the room of one of them who had pasted above his bed a sign that said 'Nothing comes between me and my chem eng'; Sizwe said to his friend, 'You must be joking, because I'm going to stay here for the next two hours, you know!' Sizwe's story thus provides a strong challenge to the stereotypical deficit view of 'disadvantage'; in his case the very coping strategies that he had developed for surviving a really challenging home environment had stood him in good stead for surviving a challenging university experience.

In closing the interview, Sizwe was asked about how he saw his prospects going forward, and his response to this question provided a transition into a new set of issues. Despite his success so far in studying engineering, Sizwe said that his real vision was to do community-oriented work, and, although he planned to get a few years' experience as a chemical engineer, he did not see himself staying in that line of work. He said that if he did stay in a corporate type job it would only be towards being able to help fund community projects.

Focus for this book

Sizwe's story touches on many key issues in contemporary higher education. At a macro level, questions around access and success continue to be prominent. Straightforwardly, these are: How can we widen the participation in higher education beyond the traditional elite? How can we increase the proportion of entrants who are able to successfully graduate? However, the story also reminds us that a simple input–output model of higher education is misguided as we also need to ask what higher education is for and whether it meets these goals. The unusualness of Sizwe's experience, where he was determined to engage broadly with the university experience, compared to that of most of his classmates, urges us to ask: What is the impact of an overloaded curriculum on student learning and on broader personal development? What, actually, are the purposes of the university degree? Should a professional degree, like engineering, include the broader focus on critical thinking and transformation of the individual that is the traditional preserve of the humanities? How should we respond to the situation of a successful engineering student feeling unease about a corporate career? How should higher education think about the role of its graduates in society?

Universities are institutions with an ancient provenance, initially conceptualised as places where only an elite portion of the population would receive a higher education, but now called to serve a much larger purpose. They are seen as the engines of social mobility and are required to work with students from a wide range of social backgrounds. As much as the central questions in higher education focus on student enrolment in programmes, student retention, progression and success, and graduate fitness for work, the actual student tends to be absent in much of this rhetoric and even in the scholarly literature. In place we have the prominence of what engineering educators even proudly term the 'pipeline metaphor' (see, for example, Schreuders et al. 2009). This technical discourse nowadays frames much of the discussion across the higher education sector. The central research questions are then of grading, selection, conversion and efficiency. These analyses have not really yielded much apart from providing indications of areas where the system is 'not working'.

Before we proceed further to consider how student learning research might be conducted, we need to step back to start to make a case in itself for the value of education research. We might agree that there are currently compelling problems and challenges in higher education, but to put our efforts into researching them is not self-evidently what we should do. It could be argued that people who are good teachers should simply focus on teaching to the best of their abilities, building a better world one graduate at a time. In fact, many of us who are higher education researchers came into the academy because we valued teaching and, similarly, many of us were recruited because of our expertise as teachers, established in the secondary school sector. Academics in the university are expected to do both teaching and research, and thus we undertook education research. Here we need to note that this is a route diametrically opposed to that taken by most of our academic colleagues, who entered the academy because they wanted to research, and then found themselves in a job that also required teaching (and we might note that it is generally assumed in the university that one does not need any special training or skills to do that).

As a community grouped together under the umbrella term of 'academic development' we have thus established ourselves as researchers: publishing in peer-reviewed journals, supervising graduate students, running funded research projects, etc. If you put your mind to it, these accomplishments are within reach of any conscientious academic. There are many good texts out there that will give great advice on the 'doing' of research into student learning – the recent book by Glynis Cousin (2009) is an excellent resource in this regard, providing a comprehensive overview of research methods and lots of sensible practical advice. For any paper you might have written there is a journal, somewhere, that will put it into print. And for any master's or doctoral thesis, there is some examiner who will give it a nod. And because our research does not generally involve specialised equipment, a lack of research funding is not necessarily an impediment. The departure point for this book is thus not to argue for *more* education research *per se*, but rather to ask hard questions about what we *are* doing in our research endeavours. South Africa is an interesting case in point. In the research arena we do more education research than just about anything else, with 10 per cent of PhDs awarded annually in this field (ASSAf 2010). Yet, on the ground, our schooling sector, on which most of this research is based, continues to lurch forward in a state of marked dysfunctionality. If we are going to take our precious time and invest it in doing research rather than teaching students, we really need to know that this is time well spent.

How, then, should higher education research proceed? This books aims to turn the contemporary conversation on its head, by inserting a full consideration of student agency into the structural context of higher education. Working sociologically, we need to understand the influence of the social context on what the individual student achieves but we also need a framework that can account for a dynamic and constantly changing external environment. Avoiding a deterministic approach, we need a way of thinking about higher education that fully accounts for individual choice and decision-making. Rather than 'measuring' their motivation and trying to correlate this or some other measured characteristic against their success in order to be able to find the perfect selection rubric, this book suggests an approach to researching student learning that takes as its starting point the student's experience. To this end, narrative data from chemical engineering students at the University of Cape Town, starting with Sizwe's story at the outset of this chapter, are used in a case study at the heart of this book to illustrate the potential value of this different approach.

Research on student learning in higher education can be seen to have originated in the late 1960s – a period when students initiated strident questioning into their experience in the university – with the publication of key studies in the USA including *The hidden curriculum* (Snyder 1971) and *Making the grade: The academic side of college life* (Becker et al. 1968). These ethnographic studies painted a fascinating picture of the disjunction between the stated aims of higher education and the actual experiences of students. On the other side of the Atlantic, towards the end of the 1970s, Noel Entwistle and colleagues at Lancaster University drew on a series of studies that had been published by Swedish researchers (Marton and Säljö 1976a, 1976b), and initiated what became an enormously influential framework for thinking about student learning: *approaches to learning*. The distinction between the 'deep' approach to learning in which students are focused towards the development of understanding and the more instrumental 'surface' approach in which the aim is to meet assessment demands, dovetailed neatly with a study that had been quite independently initiated on the other end of the globe by the Australian John Biggs, and which included a third approach, termed 'strategic' (Biggs 1978). Thus began an extraordinary expansion of research, mainly in the UK, Sweden, Australia and South Africa, exploring students' approaches to learning, and the possibilities for shifting these in what researchers considered to be more desirable directions.

In a recent review of the research on students' approaches to learning Delia Marshall and I have acknowledged that this expansive research programme has been important for shifting lecturers' attention towards the way in which students perceive their educational context (Case & Marshall 2009). A recent book by UK higher education scholar, Paul Ashwin (2009), also acknowledges this contribution, but notes too that the focus on approaches to learning has kept the field relatively confined to a particular perspective with origins in cognitive psychology. This critique builds on earlier work that also called for student learning research to take up a broader critical engagement with higher education and its social context (Malcolm & Zukas 2001; Webb 1997).

Thus this book employs a different theoretical stance. It is argued here that we cannot focus on teaching and learning in the absence of a broader understanding of the context in which these interactions take place. In much current scholarship, one can detect two extreme viewpoints: one that suggests that students, with sufficient motivation or the right learning style, can make their own success, and, on the other hand, another that claims that there is a perfect teaching method that can guarantee student success. Kevin Williams characterises this in terms of 'the twin poles of overly-individualistic, eremitical conceptions of the learner in splendid isolation from society, or of products of the hydraulic forces of society' (Williams 2012: 302). This very dilemma is something that social theorists have grappled with for a long time, and is characterised as the distinction between *structure* (the world out there) and *agency* (the person). Theories that ascribe all causality to either structure or agency have been described as 'mirror images of each other, since the one stresses complete human self-sufficiency, whilst the other emphasizes utter social dependency' (Archer 2007b: 11). There have been many different sociological theories that have attempted to explain the interaction between structure and agency in a manner that does not ascribe causal primacy to one over the other. In this book I draw on the social realist theory of the contemporary and renowned British sociologist Margaret Archer, whose life's work has focused on characterising the workings of structure and agency, and whose key emphasis is on the analytical distinctiveness of these domains.

The theoretical lens

Archer argues that alongside considerations of structure we need to place the realm of culture. *Structure* has to do with material goods (who has got the goodies, and who has not) and is also the domain of social positions and roles. *Culture* is the world of ideas and beliefs, and can be conceptualised as the contents of all the libraries in the world (Archer 1996: xvii), all possible ways of thinking about ourselves and the world we live in, both in the past and in the present. Culture includes both the worlds of propositional knowledge (in which two ideas can be put in a logical relation with each other), including science and engineering science, and the world of myths, opinions and beliefs. *Agency* is the realm of human decision and action. In an analogous way to analysing the interactions of structure and agency, Archer suggests that we need to consider the interrelationships between culture and agency.

At the heart of Archer's theory is the construct of *morphogenesis* (and its converse, morphostasis). The term morphogenesis refers to change (-genesis) in the shape of things (morpho-), a change in agency, or culture or structure. The term *morphostasis*, as the name suggests, refers to a scenario where no change takes place. The morphogenetic cycle is an analytical framework that follows the course of time. At the outset we need to note that human interactions take place in a context that has been conditioned by the twin effects of structure and culture. *Conditioning* refers to the way in which the workings of structure and culture produce constraints or enablements – although never fully deterministic – on the potential exercising of human agency. In time, the outcomes of a cycle of human interactions will produce a new conditioning for further cycles of morphogenesis or morphostasis. In understanding structural and cultural conditioning, the notion of *situational logics* is pertinent. In analysing situational logics we need to consider whether the different aspects of culture and structure are in complementary relations to each other or not. These concepts and their application in an Archerian analysis will be unpacked and applied as the book progresses.

As philosophical 'under-labourer' (Bhaskar 1998: 166), Roy Bhaskar's *critical realism* provides a crucial underpinning for Archer's social realist theory. A realist ontology conceptualises the social world as comprising distinct strata: the *actual*, the *empirical* and the *real*. Consider a first-year course. Objectively it can be observed that lectures are given at particular times of the day, that a subset of enrolled students attends the lectures, and that at the end of the course a particular pass rate is recorded. This is the level of the actual, what can be objectively observed. The focus of much student learning research has been on the range of ways in which different students perceive what is happening in the course. The level of individual subjective perceptions is termed by critical realists the empirical. (Note that these terms have particular meanings here that differ subtly from their everyday use.) What specifically interests critical realists is to develop theory that helps us characterise the level of the real. This is the non-observable world, the generative mechanisms that produce the world of human experience, both objective and subjective. It is important to emphasise here that in talking about 'mechanisms', this does not imply a simple causality, a linear cause and effect. In the social world, these mechanisms, both enabling and constraining, only have causal effects when they bump up against the intentions of individual humans.

Education is a particular social space with a distinct structural and cultural configuration. Archer's earliest work characterised the historical change in schooling systems, and her most recent piece of empirical work actually focuses on university students, but in general her theory is aimed at broad applications in social science. In order to delve deeper into what lies at the heart of the challenge of understanding student learning, in this book I build into the Archerian broader framework some key ideas from the eminent twentieth-century British sociologist of education, Basil Bernstein. His work provides a framework for thinking about the relationship between curriculum (the intended curriculum) and pedagogy (the enacted curriculum), but also for understanding how curriculum comes into existence through a *recontextualisation* of disciplinary knowledge (Bernstein 2000).

In deciding how much theory to use in this book I have been guided by Archer's own injunction to 'travel light' (Archer 1996: xiii), to use only those pieces of theory that are 'necessary and sufficient' to my purposes here. For a fuller outline of the historical development of Archer's theory and all the various competing positions, the reader is referred to her original work. In this same vein in this book I am adopting an economical approach with regard to the introduction of terminology and am only bringing in terms where they illuminate, and avoiding acronyms wherever possible!

A South African perspective

I have been researching student learning in engineering for 15 years, located in the context of post-apartheid South Africa and the attempts of universities to foster the inclusion and academic success of black[2] students, many of whom come from schooling and family backgrounds that bear the imprint of apartheid and its preceding colonial and other systems of social, economic and political exclusion. In this book I draw on narrative data emerging from a study conducted just over a decade ago with third-year chemical engineering students at the University of Cape Town. In the context of a course on advanced reactor engineering (a course I had not studied in my prior undergraduate science programme), I enrolled alongside the students in order to fully document the context. The study aimed to closely investigate the student experience of learning in this course, which had a reputation for being very challenging, but also a lecturer who was considered to be engaging and effective. It was a relatively small class, and thus when 36 of the 45 enrolled students agreed to be participants in the study, I decided to interview all of them. Two interviews were conducted with each of these students over the course of the semester. The findings of this study have been presented in a series of journal articles, a number of which were produced in collaboration with my long-term research colleague Delia Marshall from the University of the Western Cape (Case 2007; Case & Marshall 2008; Case et al. 2010; Marshall & Case 2010). In this book, narrative data from a subset of students in that study, starting with Sizwe's story that opened this chapter, are employed here towards illustrating the potential value of a social realist analysis of student learning in higher education. In preparing this book – some ten years on from the original study – I also started a process of conducting telephonic follow-up interviews with these same students, now graduates in the workplace, and these data are used to supplement those from the original study.

The South African context is wrought with particular challenges and possibilities resulting from its history of colonialism and apartheid. It is one of the most unequal societies in the world – described aptly as 'a one-nation approximation of the North–South divide' (Nixon 1994). It has a small (historically largely white but now increasingly multiracial) middle class that experiences life in many ways similar to that in high-income countries with excellent (private) healthcare and good schooling and university education. In parts of the country there is an infrastructure that is comparable to middle-income countries elsewhere in terms of roads, banking and telecommunications. Yet the majority black population of the country continues to experience the devastations of the past, with high rates of poverty and unemployment. State schooling is on many measures poorer than in other African countries. Depending on socio-economic background, South African citizens experience very different standards of healthcare. The post-apartheid democratic commitment means that the upliftment of the majority population remains a central concern.

In terms of engineering education, the context for the case study at the heart of this book, all South African undergraduate engineering qualifications are recognised internationally through the Washington Accord.[3] South African graduates take up leading positions in local and multinational firms. Although a significant proportion of South African engineering graduates are black, the country loses a disturbing number of students along the way, with success rates for black students being almost half those of white students; in a study of all students who embarked upon the four-year engineering programme at South African universities in 2001, 62 per cent of the white students had graduated after five years while only 32 per cent of black African[4] students had done so (Scott et al. 2007).

How does this speak to a global conversation on higher education? Although mindful of the need to avoid a homogenising globalised position on higher education that neglects a proper understanding of the local context (Williams 2012), I think one can note aspects in which a study of student learning in the South African context might have some relevance to other contexts elsewhere. We talk the same language since we offer degrees that are similar in broad features to those across the Anglophone world; this is especially so in the area of engineering where a measure of global comparability is established through the international mechanisms of programme accreditation. The issues around a diverse student body are also noted in many parts of the globe; in South Africa we have a pressing political imperative to transform society, and these are thus at the top of our agenda. As a country we are struggling to achieve the economic growth that we hope for, and we have an expectation that graduates should be playing a central role in fuelling this growth. We thus straddle the contexts of high- and low-income worlds in an uneasy way, but this uneasiness does sharpen the focus for the conversation. The South African context is unashamedly at the heart of this book.

At the time of writing the world is in the midst of one of the worst global recessions for decades. As a globe we are linked more than ever before not only by our interlinked economies but by our shared reliance on the very limited resources of the planet. In social terms, the economic prosperity of the last few decades in its particular patterns of distribution has served to widen, not narrow, the gap between the haves and the have-nots, across much of the global North. The predominance of serious poverty in the global South persists. What does this mean for higher education and for engineering education in particular? Our global linkages mean that we do need to have a global conversation, although maybe not in the narrow terms that we have had up until now in trumpeting an overly optimistic 'flat world' of untrammelled global capitalism (Florida 2005).

Neoliberal politics have tended to recast the purposes of higher education in restricted economic terms. A starting point for this book is a questioning of that assumption. The broader focus that is advocated is represented here by Sarah Mann's vision of the role of higher education in responding to contemporary critical challenges:

> Higher education may help to resolve some of these not by focusing on the generation of employable graduates, but by focusing on the generation of graduates capable of contributing to the huge task of tackling such challenges. Such graduates are confident, vital and resilient; inquiry driven and capable of critique, analysis and reflection; and capable of informed and reflective action in collaboration with others.
>
> (Mann 2007: 139)

This book thus deliberately attempts to be part of a global conversation, speaking from the context of the 'global South' through a particularly South African voice. My own perspective is an explicit starting point for this work. Part I attempts to create an international and historical higher education context for these enquiries as well as to locate these within contemporary movements in student learning research. Part II is where the theoretical groundwork is done, but throughout these chapters there are frequent exemplars, illustrating key theoretical ideas through reference back to student learning and higher education, particularly in the arena of engineering education. Part III is a case study of a research project conducted with chemical engineering students at the University of Cape Town; and Part IV moves to assess the potential significance of this research approach, drawing lessons from the South African case study and attempting to suggest routes forward for further student learning research in other disciplinary and national contexts. It is clear to me that the broad brushstrokes of this argument have a definite relevance across the engineering professions and further relevance into other higher education contexts, but I fully acknowledge that scholars in different disciplines will need to work out the details in their own contexts. The book aims merely to contribute towards a growing and dynamic area of scholarship, rather than attempting in any way to have the last word.

Making values explicit

Research is aimed towards generating knowledge. Is all research based on the same ways of knowing? In exploring the possibilities for a reinvigorated and more productive social science, the Danish scholar Bent Flyvbjerg (2001) goes back to an early typology from the work of Aristotle: *episteme*, *techne* and *phronesis*. *Episteme* is the way of producing knowledge that has driven the extraordinary developments in our modern society. It aims towards findings that are predictive, universal and context-independent. *Techne*, from which we get our word 'technology', refers to the creation of artefacts. It is a pragmatic and context-dependent enterprise. A further pragmatic and context dependent form of knowledge is *phronesis*, for which 'ethics' is a poor and limited modern translation. Flyvbjerg argues that the limited value of much contemporary social science is due to its captivation with *episteme* and its relative undervaluing of *phronesis*. To give a sense of the fuller space in which *phronesis* operates, here are the kind of questions that would drive a search for knowledge that is oriented towards *phronesis*:

- Where are we going?
- Is this desirable?
- What should be done?

(Flyvbjerg 2001: 60)

In thus stating that the significant questions in higher education are not only those of efficiency but also questions on the purposes of higher education, this book is arguing for an inclusion of *phronesis* into education research.

This, then, also implies a normative stance, with a judgement on the world we are in and some idea of where we would like to be. Andrew Sayer (2005), a prominent critical realist scholar, notes how over the last 200 years social science has worked to purge the normative from its explicit modes of working. He calls for a return to a blending of the positive and the normative in order to work sensibly with the issues of the day. Even lay debates of higher education tend to be located within some kind of view on 'how things could be improved'. In many such places, though, the particular normative position is not made explicit. This book works with a particular view on social justice. The ultimate arbiter of 'what way is up' is considered to be a space that can offer opportunities for human flourishing across all members of the human race, as so clearly expressed in the work of South African education scholar Melanie Walker (see, for example, Walker 2010). We have a long way to go in terms of achieving this dream. But we do know what it means, particularly for those of us, most probably all the readers of this book, who have built lifestyles where we are able to pursue our interests and our commitments; where the basics of life, such as food and shelter, are fully assured. This book uses a stance that as a human race we need to broaden access to those opportunities across the human population. This position has been most significantly elaborated in the work of Nobel Prize-winning Indian economist, Amartya

Sen, whose economic theories centred on the possibilities for human flourishing across whole populations (Sen 1999).

To work through the role of higher education in promoting broad social good is not a simple matter, and is one that will be taken up in the next chapter. At this point what needs to be stated is that we can all imagine a world that could be better than the one we currently live in and that higher education, as an enterprise in which society makes a huge investment, should have a crucial role towards the fulfilment of that dream. Sayer (2005) makes the point clearly that we need to move beyond simplistic critiques of capitalism: the complex society that we live in makes a return to an agrarian past not possible or desirable. At present we do not have better models for knowing how to organise national and global economic activity other than the complex division of labour that the basic structure of capitalist activity offers. However, it can be noted that over the history of capitalism it has demonstrated a range of different forms in particular times and places – capitalism *per se* does not imply a particular level of inequality within society. We operate currently in a space where the unfettered workings of the market were assumed to be all we need and we have seen the serious outworkings of that naïve belief. In global protests we can recognise a wish to build a more responsible form of government that protects society from these kinds of man-made disasters.

As much as this book looks towards the future it also adopts the perspective offered by the sociologist Rob Moore (2009), who argues against the danger of 'schismatic thinking' that has characterised much work to date in the sociology of education. This is a perspective that 'authorizes itself through the proclamation of a radical break with some mainstream, "dominant" or "conventional" body of knowledge that is held to be hegemonic and, in many cases, also oppressive' (p. 120). Rather, with a social realist perspective we should be able to work within a space which the philosopher Randall Collins (2000) terms 'in media res, in the middle of things'. This is a perspective where we understand the complex world in which we live, the past that conditions the present, as well as the range of interactions in the present that will produce the future. There is no space here for some idealistic or utopian future but rather a careful sense of small possibilities for change and progress that are grounded in a sense of the mechanisms that causally influence our lives in emergent ways. Sayer notes: 'Realists . . . seek to identify both necessity and possibility or potential in the world – what things must go together, and what can happen, given the nature of objects' (2000: 11).

Outline of the book

Archer's notion of morphogenesis, as awkward as that term is, provides the guiding orientation for this book. What sort of changes are we interested in seeing in the arena of higher education? Centrally, we are focused on the morphogenesis of student agency; for students to leave higher education with different knowledge and capacity for action than that with which they entered. This is a relatively tight cycle taking place over a few years. How do we respond to the call for an 'ontological' turn that focuses attention on student 'being'? In this book we are also concerned to understand the possibilities for change within our domains, whether engineering education or another disciplinary domain. This will be a longer-term process, taking place over the career spans of academics and other key players, even though this can, of course, be influenced by the agency of individuals and groups of students. Thus we can summarise as follows two key questions that drive the exploration throughout this book:

1. What changes in student agency might be considered desirable outcomes for higher education?
2. How will the system need to change (structurally and culturally) to better enable the kinds of changes in student agency that are desired?

Part I sets the scene for the book, starting in Chapter 1 with an overview of the global context of higher education. This moves in Chapter 2 into a consideration of student learning research, working from a common-sense view on researching education through to developing a view on why a theory that allows for an understanding of the interplay between structure and agency might be needed.

Part II sets up the theoretical orientation for the book. Readers who are already familiar with contemporary discussions in higher education might choose to skip directly to this section. First, in Chapter 3, critical realism is outlined as a perspective that offers an important ontological and epistemological foundation. This is followed in Chapter 4 by an overview of key concepts in the work of Archer, focusing on her distinctive conceptualisation of structure, culture and agency, moving through to the notion of situational logics that explain the possibilities for morphogenesis or morphostasis. The next important theoretical angle, presented in Chapter 5, is a realist perspective on knowledge and curriculum, building particularly on the work of Bernstein. Finally, in Chapter 6, these theories are drawn together to provide a focus on the development of student agency.

Part III is a case study on student learning in the chemical engineering programme at the University of Cape Town, and the context for this study is given in Chapter 7. Chapter 8 sketches the context of engineering education, both its contemporary concerns and its historical origins. A particular focus is on understanding the kinds of progressive visions that are currently at play in both higher education and engineering education. The book will engage closely with these possibilities in terms of understanding what it might take to change the system in particular ways, both to allow for a broader range of student participation and success, and to enable a broader vision of the purposes of an engineering degree and its potential contribution to society. This chapter is likely to appeal especially to fellow engineering educators, and others may well choose to speed on to the narratives that follow.

The remainder of Part III presents an analysis of narrative data in this case study. Noting the significance of temporality in the morphogenetic cycle, Chapter 9 starts the clock ticking by considering the student's choice to study engineering.

This is the first aspect of contemporary concerns about engineering education – who is enrolling – and this chapter offers a way of analysing student choice that is in line with a full regard for agency, focusing particularly on modes of reflexivity. Chapter 10 concentrates on the experience of being an engineering student, responding to the second contemporary concern, which is for student success in engineering. Here, Archer's model of personal identity is used to understand what it is that engineering studies demand of the student. Chapter 11 expands this model of identity into social identity, which is used as a basis for looking at students' engagements with peers and educators. Chapter 12 dwells further on students' engagement with their engineering studies, with a focus on what is termed here 'the knowledge project'. Drawing in further tools from Bernstein, in this chapter the engineering curriculum and its structural and cultural impacts are considered in detail. Chapter 13 draws together the analysis of these narratives, and on this basis argues for an enlarged space for the morphogenesis of student agency in this programme.

The final section of the book, Part IV, considers the implications of the analysis of student learning through the lens of social realism, and what this means for the possibilities for progressive change of the system. This analysis in Chapter 14 is located within an understanding of the crucial structural and cultural impediments to such morphogenesis. The chapter then moves to consider the implications of this perspective on student learning for engineering education and higher education more generally.

Notes

1   All student names in this book are pseudonyms. This particular case study was written up in an earlier article where the pseudonym Mandla was used; here it has been changed to Sizwe to avoid any confusion for an international audience who might wonder at the reasons for using a name that could seem close to that of (Nelson) Mandela. (Marshall, D. & Case, J.M. (2010) 'Rethinking "disadvantage" in higher education: A paradigmatic case study using narrative analysis', *Studies in Higher Education*, 35. 491–504.)

2   This term is used throughout the book to refer to all racial groups that were discriminated against under apartheid; those termed black African, 'coloured' (what internationally is usually referred to as 'mixed race') and Indian. The perpetuation of racial categorisation does not reflect any belief in the inherent biological reality of race, but rather recognises that race as a social construct continues to influence advantage and disadvantage today. The pseudonyms that have been chosen for students reflect the diversity of 'blackness' in South Africa, with indigenous African names for students who would be characterised as 'black African' and English names for those previously classified as 'coloured', as is relatively typical in contemporary South Africa.

3   The Washington Accord is an international system of mutual accreditation of four-year engineering degrees. Signatories to the Washington Accord are Australia, Canada, Chinese Taipei, Hong Kong China, Ireland, Japan, Korea, Malaysia, New Zealand, Singapore, South Africa, Turkey, UK and USA (http://www.washingtonaccord.org/).

4   With small sample sets for 'coloured' and Indian students, this study chose to contrast mainly white with black African success rates.

Part I

Setting the scene

The educational literature – both popular and serious – is full of rhetoric. Some accounts offer a golden past. What all offer is a contemporary state of crisis and the need for radical change. How can we think our way through all of this? Here an attempt is made to locate the current debates in higher education both historically and philosophically. In Chapter 1 a measured argument is made for how we might think of contemporary challenges in higher education, and the potential value, therefore, of student learning research. This then moves in Chapter 2 into a consideration about how such research might be conducted, arguing for the limitations of approaches that focus either purely on context (in a deterministic form) or on the individual (equally deterministic but unrelated to anything else). The conclusion is that a sophisticated sociological approach will be needed in order to do justice to the demands for a nuanced and productive line of research in this field.

Chapter 1

Contemporary challenges in higher education

There is a vibrant scholarship currently engaged with higher education, in both its international and South African contexts, and this chapter cannot hope to do justice to the full scope of those arguments. Towards the purposes of this book, however, salient issues will be outlined in this chapter.

The contemporary global higher education landscape

The global landscape of higher education has seen dramatic changes over the last relatively short period of time. On a growth trajectory since the middle of the twentieth century, participation in higher education continues to expand, now at an inexorable pace in contexts like India and China but with steady pressure everywhere. In 1970, there were just over 28 million students enrolled in higher education across the globe, with 75 per cent of these in the wealthy West. By 2006, with the world's population having nearly doubled, the number of students in higher education had increased just over five times to nearly 144 million. At this point just over 40 per cent of these students were in the West (Unterhalter & Carpentier 2010). And this growth trajectory has been exponential over this period, with nearly half of the absolute growth over this period happening in the first few years of the new century. A key contemporary scholar who documents and analyses these trends is the Australian, Simon Marginson, and his work will be drawn on extensively in the discussion that follows.

Reflecting during the 1970s on the post-war growth in participation in higher education in Western democracies, an American scholar, Martin Trow, intro duced a conceptual framework that has had enduring utility (Trow 2006), distinguishing between the traditional *elite* systems, which take under 15 per cent of the age cohort into higher education and a *mass* higher education, which works with a larger and broader group. Once participation is beyond 50 per cent, Trow describes this as a *universal* system. Significantly, Trow suggests that these different systems, by virtue of the proportion of the population in their intake, tend to be related with different functions. Elite higher education, working with a highly selective group, has changed from a focus on producing the 'cultivated gentleman' but still works with a group that have ambitions to be leaders in society, and these universities are set up to nurture these ambitions. Mass systems tend to be focused more on skills and preparation for particular vocational roles – by definition one cannot assume that up to 50 per cent of the age cohort will become leaders in society. Of course, elite institutions can and still do exist within a broader system that has mass participation. Once a country has higher education participation beyond 50 per cent, graduateness is no longer an assurance of anything special – Trow argues that in these cases, where university participation becomes similar to school participation, the system is geared towards adapting a whole population to a context of rapid change.

It is hardly surprising that in most places the growth in student numbers with a move away from elite participation towards mass and even universal participation has not been matched with a concomitant growth in state resource. Even in countries in South East Asia where dramatic growth in higher education has been largely state-directed, increasingly there is an expectation on students and their families to be contributing towards the cost of their studies (Marginson 2011). In many countries, universities are now required to achieve more with less state resource. This has been particularly notable in parts of the industrialised world where a set of government policies focused towards the welfare state made way in the 1980s for the harsh dictates of neo-liberalism. The paradigmatic case here is the UK, where in recent times there has been a rapid departure from full state funding of higher education towards a system driven by student fees. In low-income countries, state funding for higher education has typically not been able to keep pace with the exploding demand, and in many contexts private providers have moved in swiftly. The international movement of students from poor countries to obtain qualifications in rich countries is a largely post-war phenomenon, which has further intensified in recent times: between 1995 and 2004 the number of students studying outside their country of citizenship increased from 1.3 million to 2.7 million (Marginson 2008).

Higher education has truly become a global phenomenon in many respects. Marginson (2006: 57), recognising a radical increase in cross-national flows of staff and students, knowledge and ideas, states that 'For the first time in history we can talk about "the university" in terms of not just a national field but a global field.' We are all aware of the dramatic technological advances that have made this possible – most notably in the area of networked communications and computer power, but also in the availability of relatively cheap air travel. Marginson also cautions, however, that we need to recognise that despite these changes on the global level there remains considerable national and indeed local variation in higher education. We need to avoid simplistic arguments and recognise that the changes we see in higher education, indeed its transformation in global terms, is 'never so complete, nor solely engineered from above by managers and governments, let alone cosmic forces of "capitalism" and "globalisation"' (Marginson 2006: 46).

Those of us living in the Anglophone world need particularly to note that the way we tend to talk about higher education, especially our obsession with international rankings and our implicit valorisation of a Harvard/Oxbridge model, is maybe not as widespread as we might assume. Marginson (2006) challenges these normative assumptions by lifting out exemplars from elsewhere, such as UNAM in Mexico, which has 270,000 students and only recently started being selective in admission but which is also one of the world's top research universities. The massive growth in higher education in South East Asia is also likely in the future to provide a strong challenge to Western ideas on higher education (Marginson 2011).

Rethinking the purposes of higher education

In contemporary times the economic arguments for the value and purposes of higher education have become increasingly salient. Marginson identifies the drivers:

> Intensified status competition, locking neatly into neo-liberal government, is reconstituting the field of higher education (Bourdieu, 1988) as a competitive market in private status goods. This, not a structural transformation consequent on changes in scale, is decisive.
>
> (Marginson 2006: 44)

The so-called 'knowledge economy' predicates economic growth on the production of appropriately skilled graduates. For the individual there has been a promise of higher earnings following an investment in higher education, but in the post-industrialised West that contract is increasingly broken (Brown et al. 2011). In middle- and low-income countries, the last two decades have seen a massive international policy shift, from a position where the World Bank and others decreed that school education should be prioritised over higher education, to a situation where higher education is now seen as the panacea to a range of societal and economic challenges.

A trenchant criticism of a narrow conception of the purposes of higher education, linking education too closely to employability, and economic growth too closely to broad social well-being, can be found in the work of American philosopher, Martha Nussbaum. Drawing on the work of Sen, she argues for a broader understanding of the relationship between higher education and human development (Nussbaum 2010). Crucially, she argues that a view of national progress that focuses solely, for example, on average Gross Domestic Product (GDP), can mask massive inequities in society. To advance in GDP terms, a nation need only educate a small technical elite. Importantly, to achieve this successfully, that small elite should not be exposed too much to critical thinking or indeed to any views that might have them questioning the basis for economic development. To illustrate these dangers, she draws on work in the Indian state of Gujarat, which has achieved massive technological and economic progress, but where many parts of that society remain destitute. She notes that in her perspective it is not a choice between economic development or human development, but rather that the broader view on human development also encompasses economic development.

To be able to find our way through this minefield we need a careful consideration and restatement of what the purposes of higher education might be. Noting again the differentiation across the sector both within and across countries, we need to know how to ask this question. South African sociologist and scholar of higher education, Saleem Badat, cautions well against a functionalist approach:

> The meaning of higher education and universities cannot be found in the content of their teaching and research, how they undertake these, or their admission policies. Instead, the core purposes of higher education and universities reside elsewhere.
>
> (Badat 2009: 4)

Drawing on contemporary scholarship, Badat (2011) asserts two core purposes for higher education:

1. The production of knowledge – which advances understanding of the natural and social worlds, and enriches humanity's accumulated scientific and cultural inheritances and heritage.
2. The dissemination of knowledge – and the formation and cultivation of the cognitive character of students.

With regard to the so-called 'third mission' of the university, community engagement, Badat (2011) grapples with whether this is a third purpose or not but resolves that it is better seen as a role that needs to be in alignment with the two purposes; it is not a purpose in and of itself for the university.

A key issue at stake is whether the purposes of the university should be primarily oriented towards public or private goods. Marginson (2006), although acknowledging that these are concepts that have shifted over time, responds to this debate by drawing on classic liberal theory, which distinguishes between individual and collective goods. On this basis public goods are defined as (i) non-rivalrous, i.e. they can be consumed by any number of people without being depleted, and (ii) non-excludable, i.e. the benefits cannot be confined to individual buyers. On this basis it can be argued that university education and research, meeting most of these characteristics, are 'part-public' goods. It is also true that university education does confer private goods on individual graduates in their potential income and other benefits post-graduation, but the argument here is that to confine the purposes of universities to this outcome is to sell them very short. Even the view that sees the public good as the cumulative outcomes of many individual private goods is limited, as is that which confines public good to a consideration of economic public good.

There is a growing corpus of work in higher education scholarship, then, that is developing a nuanced and detailed understanding of the 'public good' purposes of higher education. A recent book by British scholar, Jon Nixon (2011), focuses on the ways in which the capacities that universities seek to develop in their students can be conceptualised as benefiting the public good. He summarises these as three core capacities, viz. (i) capability, (ii) reasoning together and (iii) purposefulness. Human capability theory, developed by Walker (2010) and based on the work of Sen and Nussbaum, is employed here by Nixon towards a perspective that focuses on students being able to 'to gather their abilities and achievements, their gifts and talents, their failures and disappointments, and make of them lives that are worthwhile both for themselves and others' (p. 83). Collective human reasoning is going to become increasingly important as a capacity for the survival of our species in the context of a resource crisis, yet we can note that higher education as currently constituted focuses almost exclusively on individual achievement. With regard to purposefulness, Nixon notes our current 'back-to-front' ontology, where school leavers are required to work out 'what they want to be', and then almost work backwards from that projected future. In its stead, Nixon emphasises figuring out what you want to *do* with your life, an ongoing process of 'working our lives forward'.

To avoid being caught between the limitations of a functionalist approach or indeed what some might term an idealist approach, we need to go back to consider what it is that makes the university a distinct form, a particular space where certain things are possible that are not possible in other societal institutions. Here, the work of French sociologist Pierre Bourdieu has great relevance, as summarised by Marginson (2006: 51): 'Bourdieu's insight was that the autonomy of universities has enabled them to evolve distinctive forms of inner life and modes of social value.' Bourdieu's understanding of the university as a field allows us to account both for the way it deals with the external world, refracting external demands and thus modifying them into forms that suit its own inner logic (Maton 2005). A recent PhD study by Bruce Kloot shows how South African universities have refracted pressures from the external political environment to produce foundation programmes that both satisfy (to some extent) these external pressures as well as leaving the core workings of the university unchanged (Kloot 2011).

Marginson neatly summarises this as follows:

> What makes universities socially distinctive is that they are self-reproducing, knowledge-forming organizations. They are defined by the binary between the known and the unknown. No other social or economic institution is defined *primarily* by this binary, although a growing number take it into their operation.
>
> (Marginson 2007: 126)

Moving further in a Bourdieuian vein, Marginson notes how, while sociologists have focused their attention on the capacity of universities to foster (or not) upward social mobility (in economic terms), there has between little attention to what he terms 'geographical' and 'cultural' mobility. A university degree will not necessarily guarantee a high-paying job in contemporary times, especially in societies with massified higher education systems, but a good degree should expand horizons and allow for an ability to function outside one's natal context. In this regard he makes the pointed observation that universities are actually 'much more effective and generative in horizontal mobility than vertical mobility' (Marginson 2006: 55).

The roles of the academic

The contemporary emphasis on research output of individual academics can to some extent be traced back to the dramatic expansion in funding of (science) research at universities in the post-World War II period, especially in the USA. This started a noted shift in the academy in terms of expectations of the activities of academic staff members. At the same time the dramatic growth in graduate enrolments led to a large potential pool of academic staff who already had research careers underway, with PhDs and often post-doc experience in hand. With some contextual variation we have now come to a point where across the globe research is a highly valued activity, and not only for the intrinsic benefits of knowledge creation – it is an attractive source of income for increasingly cash-strapped institutions.

Kloot's (2011) study traces the situational logics that condition the space for academic work, using as case studies the engineering faculties at the University of Cape Town and the historically Afrikaans-medium Stellenbosch University. Through a detailed analysis working within a Bourdieuian framework, he shows how activities related to research are privileged in both of these institutional contexts. This is characterised in Bourdieu's terms as 'intellectual capital' and is a form of power, operating in the international arena, that carries more weight than the 'academic capital', which is related to the day-to-day running of the university and its undergraduate programme. Kloot's study shows that the work of academic development runs counter to this logic. He shows how individuals at UCT were relatively successful in carving out a space for academic development, more so than a parallel enterprise at Stellenbosch University, but that even at UCT this remains a contested space.

As much as one can argue for the logical and important links between teaching and research, it must be acknowledged that these do largely define different spheres of activity for academics with different time scales and calendars (Rowland 1996). The teaching calendar runs on a semester and annual basis, with distinct times when contact with undergraduates through lecturing or other activities is demanded. There is the associated time of preparation and marking during these periods. The research calendar is different, even when some aspects of budgeting might run annually. For academics who do not live in the northern hemisphere, the summer international conference season falls right in the middle of teaching. With regard to supervision of research students, although some aspects of supervision can be scheduled weekly in a similar manner to lectures, there will be intensive activities that require substantial chunks of time, for example, when a final draft of a PhD thesis requires comment. When funders visit and report deadlines are due, the situational logics of a space that valorises research above all else requires that all else is dropped. Lectures are cancelled or given by graduate students, tests do not get marked timeously, and students seeking help are brushed away from the office.

The silos of individual courses mean that to some extent these conflicting requirements get managed in the traditional curriculum. Individual lecturers are able to work out idiosyncratic accommodations of the various demands in their day, although maybe not always with full success. However, when curriculum arrangements demand that lecturers collaborate to offer an integrated course such as a design project, the situational logics mean that we should not be surprised when we see pedagogical commitments falling apart, such as was noted by Linda Kotta's (2011) study of a design course that had been constructed to take students step by step through the design process with interim feedback along the way. The design course was intended to draw on knowledge that was being taught in two courses running in parallel. The lecturers involved had great intentions, but in the busyness of their academic lives both these aspects fell apart. Students were not given interim feedback in sufficient time in order to utilise it in their final submissions, and the lecturers teaching in the parallel courses were not sufficiently appraised of the details of the design course in order to be able to sequence the material in their courses appropriately. The impact on students was significant, with even academically successful students not feeling sure about whether they had done the right thing, and most other students floundering.

The significance of professional education

The older professions of medicine and law are as old as the university itself. Thus professional education has always been an important part of higher education. Engineering education entered the academy in the nineteenth century, and this story is taken up in more detail in Part III of this book. At this point, thinking more generally about higher education, it is important to revisit the role of professional education, particularly as it pertains to contemporary challenges. The American scholar, William Sullivan, argues for a reclaiming of the ideals of professionalism in contemporary times.

> At its worst, professionalism can lock individuals into a narrow focus upon technical competence (and sometimes individual success) to the exclusion of all other considerations. At its best, however, professionalism is far more than that. By taking responsibility through one's work for ends of social importance, an individual's skills and aspirations acquire value for others.
>
> (Sullivan 2004: 30)

In the context of engineering education, as one would expect, the general discourse on engineering education is focused more towards the overall needs of the economy and less on the importance of engineering education for individual enhancement, although that motivation does come into play when considering the reasons that individual students might choose to do engineering. Significantly, it might be noted that engineering has for some time been a route into the middle class, and continues to be so for individual students (Becker 2010). On aggregate we might note that engineering education in this sense could be argued to play an important role in fostering social mobility, although with the relatively low success rates, particularly for students from less advantaged backgrounds, these effects are muted to some degree.

Sullivan (2004) provides a far more wide-ranging conceptualisation of the role of engineering education within a contemporary understanding of the significance of professional education. He notes that the post-war period saw a contraction of purpose across a range of professional programmes, focusing more sharply on technical and scientific knowledge. Notwithstanding the enormous power of significant advances on this front, he argues that contemporary times have shown that the neglect of the broader dimensions of a professional education have placed the role of the professional in society to some degree in crisis. This has been most vividly noted in the financial arenas, where the ethical commitment that one might have expected from graduate professionals has been shown to be sorely lacking in a number of cases.

Access and success

Badat (2009) builds on a broad contemporary understanding of the purposes of higher education, encompassing a sophisticated notion of the public good, to argue for the specific roles of the universities, noting that these roles derive from an understanding of the university's location in a particular social context. He offers an engaging list:

a. To cultivate highly educated people.
b. To contribute to forging a critical and democratic citizenship.
c. To engage with the development needs and challenges of our societies.
d. To engage with the intellectual and cultural life of societies.
e. To imaginatively and creatively undertake different types of rigorous scholarship and rigorous research.

With regard to the first key aim towards the cultivation of 'highly educated people', central to the focus of this book – student learning – Badat notes of course that we need to produce graduates who can function effectively in a dynamic and challenging world:

> Our programmes must enable our students to graduate as professionals who can think theoretically and imaginatively; gather and analyse information

with rigour; critique and construct alternatives and communicate effectively orally and in writing.

(Badat 2009: 7)

However, Badat also emphasises that coupled here has to be a commitment – because of an overall commitment to social equity – to enable students from a broad range of social backgrounds to obtain what Morrow (2009) has termed 'epistemological access'.

For foundational thinking in this regard we can also draw productively on the work of the sociologist of education, Bernstein, who identifies what he terms three pedagogical rights. The first is the right to individual enhancement:

> Enhancement is not simply the right to be *more* personally, *more* intellectually, *more* socially, *more* materially, it is the right to the means of critical understandings and to new possibilities.

(Bernstein 2000: xx)

The second pedagogical right is 'the right to be included socially, intellectually, culturally and personally', while the third right is that to participate in democratic processes – 'where order is constructed, maintained and changed' (Bernstein 2000: 7).

These are what Bernstein considers fundamental rights of the student for any education system. Whether we are talking about a selective elite institution or a country with mass participation in higher education, there is no point in taking in a student if the institution is not able to provide the context in which they can flourish educationally.

The possibilities and challenges of new technology

In the realm of communication technologies we live in an era of dramatic and fast-paced change. The argument that computer technology has the potential to radically change education has been around now for many decades. Over this period we have of course seen some changes – course websites, online retrieval of journal articles, widespread use of email – but up to now one could say that nothing yet has been a real 'game-changer' in terms of the basic structure of higher education. These tools have certainly been useful but follow a long line of educational tools such as the photocopier and the overhead projector – used by professors and students in largely face-to-face contexts. The arguments suggesting the potential for radical change have been in the arena of online education, so-called 'e-learning'. Here it is suggested that the internet has the potential to completely transform the form of higher education systems. To date, there has been some development in the arena of traditional distance learning, now largely supplemented with online communication, and a considerable development at the postgraduate level, particularly in taught master's degrees and other offerings for full-time professionals to further their education. But at the undergraduate level, around the world, higher education has largely retained its face-to face-format, supplemented with some online provision of materials and electronic forms of communication.

A very recent development in the form of MOOCs – Massive Open Online Content – is argued to have the potential to be the real 'game-changer' (Marginson 2012). Over the last few years the technology has been developed and has been taken up by some high-profile, largely US universities, to put content online and to allow for large numbers of people to sign up online, free, and to actually take courses, some of which – following a payment – give the possibility of certified outcomes (following automated quiz-based assessment). At this stage, there are limited possibilities for taking a full degree in this mode, and the funding models are uncertain, but the educational technology community is atwitter with discussion about the possibilities.

The challenge is timely. Residential university education is extremely costly, and if all it is going to offer is something that can be done through a MOOC – presumably low-level mastery of basic content – then it is going to get a run for its money. But the position put forward in this chapter on the purposes of higher education suggests an institution that rests on intensive engagement by its students, and it is likely this will continue to involve face-to-face contact between academics and students, even if this is cleverly supported by the best possible uses of online tools. This will be especially true at the undergraduate level, where students have exited school and are meeting an educational context that for many of them will require a different form of learning from that which they have experienced at school. Although we are likely to see a massive proliferation of opportunities for post-school learning in the very near future, this book adopts a tight definition of what a *true* higher education is about, and this forms the backdrop for the examination of student learning that is to follow.

In summary

The dramatic increase in participation in higher education in individual countries and globally is a significant structural change that has brought with it a wake of challenges and possibilities. One key issue is that the traditional means whereby society has funded higher education have generally been strained. This tension has precipitated a strident questioning of the purposes of higher education. In this context, where increasingly the purposes of higher education are represented in instrumental terms, this chapter has drawn on key scholars to provide a position that focuses towards a much broader notion of societal well-being, and the distinctive role of universities in promoting this end. This also links to an enlarged perspective on professional education, also aimed crucially towards developing professionals who can address key challenges that society faces in contemporary times.

A more diverse student intake has also raised questions about what might be assumed as reasonable preparation for higher education, and what challenges contemporary students will face in coming to grips with the knowledge demands of university study. Universities can no longer assume an elite and uniform intake, even those who continue to embody the elite functions of preparing leaders for the future. Key challenges are in the area of facilitating success for students from a broad range of social backgrounds.

Technology continues to hold itself out as a panacea to a wide range of ills – contemporary developments put themselves out as the ultimate 'game-changers'. Working off the understanding of the purposes of higher education established here, it is possible to see that, although universities need to make the best uses of current technological tools, fully automated online programmatic course environments are unlikely at this point to be able to offer the kind of educational outcomes that are desirable.

In this context, then, the potential contribution of student learning research is important. We cannot work off traditional assumptions about our students and their place in society, where they come from and where they are going to. We are right to question afresh how we are using the precious resources of our salaries and their time, to contribute towards society something that is at least partly a public good. With this backdrop we then move to consider how we might undertake research in student learning.

Chapter 2

Researching student learning

Accounting for structure and agency

If we agree that there are real and pressing challenges in higher education and that research might assist in identifying productive routes of action for addressing these, then we need to think about how we might go about doing research in education. This chapter considers various ways of doing education research and starts building the argument for a more sociologically informed approach.

Contemporary approaches to researching education

Many people who teach in universities assume that it must be pretty straightforward to do education research. Those who are trained in scientific research might assume that the methods for researching the natural world might easily translate into research on the social world. Education is a phenomenon in the social world. We are not dealing with bridges or power stations but with human beings and their engagement with knowledge. How we think about this world is a crucial determinant of what we can know about this world. In the next chapter we will dig deeper into questions of ontology – what the world is – but for now we need to do some groundwork in the area of epistemology – considering different approaches to how we can come to know about this world, particularly if the phenomenon under consideration is education. Two key paradigms that have guided much research to date, and which will be discussed here, are summarised in Table 2.1.

Given the valorisation of dominant modes of doing scientific research in the academy, there is often a desire to produce objective knowledge that is quantifiable and testable. Many such scholars feel drawn towards identifying variables and attempting to test the relationships between them. In the social science world this perspective on research is often (pejoratively) labelled 'positivist', but a more

Table 2.1 Two research paradigms in education

Research paradigm	Focusing on	Aimed towards
Empiricism	Objective measurements	Prediction
Interpretivism	Subjective experiences	Understanding

useful (and less loaded) umbrella term is *empiricism*. It should be acknowledged here that we have found out some important things about student learning in education from these explorations. We have a fairly good idea of who our students are, and we know, for example, that women's participation in engineering education in most programmes around the world sits at well below the 50 per cent of their demographic representation in society (Schreuders et al. 2009). We also know – as has been proved again and again in just about any educational context – that one of the best predictors of students' future academic success is their past academic performance (for example, Smith 2012). This research has helped us to identify areas that we need to explore further, but in and of itself research has not been able to do so. It is noted – hardly surprisingly – that students who, for example, check 'strongly agree' against a statement that describes them as motivated to study are also those who persist and perform in the degree. There are, of course, also myriad problems associated with students' interpretations of items in quantitative inventories of learning approaches (Mogashana et al. 2012).

Some work in this vein looks for technical solutions to improve the outcomes of education systems, focusing on teaching methods as a simple matter of technique. Thus, in a similar way to testing a new drug by its assignment to an experimental group and a placebo to a control group, we can assign students to different classrooms where different teaching methods are in operation, and we can compare the academic performance of these two groups (for example, Hsieh & Knight 2008). Many claims have been made on the basis of such studies, and some of them seem to hint at possible truths, but overall they leave us with too many questions. Context is simply too bedevilling, both in terms of the difficulty of creating matched samples of students, as well as the difficulty of identifying to what extent other extraneous variables are at play. Introducing an innovation and testing its effects always opens up the possibility of the much-debated 'Hawthorne effect' (Wickström & Bendix 2000), where an innovation can produce positive results in the short term simply owing to a natural human propensity to respond positively to a changed environment. A plethora of studies has generated complicated statistics certifying the validity of various correlations, but typically these studies are not able to tell us how we might go about attempting to change the status quo; how we can actually change the system of education so that we might obtain different outcomes. We also end up knowing comparatively little about the students in our programmes, their motivations, how their studies fit into their broader lives, and how they juggle the challenges of the programme.

Research on student learning has stepped into this gap. Here we have work that focuses squarely on the student. From the field of psychology we have a range of constructs with which we can characterise student learning, many of them quantifiable. Thus, we can measure motivation, personality traits, learning styles, and so on. A major shift in social science over the last few decades was the development of trustworthy qualitative methods along with the formulation of *interpretivism* as a research paradigm. Here we shift from trying to make objective measurements of a phenomenon towards trying to understand the phenomenon subjectively from the point of view of the individuals involved. We can identify a range of different ways in which, say, being an engineering student, is perceived. There are now many studies that give us important perspectives on how the curriculum functions, not only as defined by the lecturer but, crucially, as experienced by the student. We have managed to get a student's view on the degree of overload in the curriculum, and we have started to understand the ways in which women and students of colour can feel included or excluded in our programmes (for example, Tate & Linn 2005; Seymour 1995).

The limitation of such work, however, is that we are still left with little sense of how we may proceed to improve what we do. Such studies certainly go a long way in building empathy among some educators and offering some insights into the different perceptions held by students in their classes, but are limited in giving us a bigger sense of how the system functions and identifying the constraints on progress. To move beyond wishful thinking, we need the tools in order to be able to 'specify under what conditions we are condemned to reproduce our culture versus which conditions allow us the freedom to transform it' (Archer 1996: xxv).

Starting to think sociologically: structure and agency

Education is a social process; it is much more than the individual and the processes in the individual mind. Bhaskar has noted how ridiculous it would be to attempt a purely individualistic, that is, non-social account of human behaviour (Bhaskar 1989). To properly understand the very real influence of context on the education process, we need to engage with sociology. When we note that women or people of colour are experiencing higher education in particular ways, we will not go very far if we limit our explorations to a description of individual experience. These phenomena are social phenomena, and we will only develop plausible social theories if we engage with both the social dimensions of education and also its broader location within society.

The literature on approaches to learning has made some important moves in this direction, characterising these approaches not as fixed characteristics of the individual, but rather as emergent from the context. Approaches to learning are a coming together of students' prior experiences and their perceptions of the current context. There are a number of limitations in this work, however. First, what do we mean by 'context'? Here, the well-known student learning scholar, Paul Ramsden (2003), offers us a list including assessment, course and institutional context, but it is difficult to know how to operationalise this further. In my own attempts I could come, for example in my research on second-year students, to a position where it was clear how a time-stressed course and assessment environment tended to militate against students' abilities to adopt a deep approach (Case & Gunstone 2003), but it did not allow for the building of a more elaborate explanatory theory. Another problem with the theorisation of approaches to learning is that, because of its weak approach to context, it tends to be generally misinterpreted as a theory speaking only to student characteristics.

How do we even start to take account more effectively for the social context in which student learning takes place? Fortunately, sociologists have been grappling with this for a long time. We are talking about the interactions between the 'parts' (society) and the 'people'. The terms *structure* and *agency* are generally used to signal these distinct aspects of social life.

Structure refers to different roles in society and the institutions that sustain them. At the heart of structural arrangements is the differential distribution of material resources in society. This then also refers to the other demographic markers that condition life chances: the workings of race, class and gender.

Agency is the space where the individual acts with intentionality – the actions of a person. Archer notes that there is no time where both structure and agency are not 'jointly in play' (Archer 2008: 465). We know this from our personal experience. Archer writes: 'For it is part and parcel of daily experience to feel both free and enchained, capable of shaping our own future and yet confronted by towering, seemingly impersonal, constraints' (Archer 1996: xii).

Although we have this merged and conjoined experience of the world, to be able to advance explanatory theory we need to analytically separate the workings of structure and agency. Moreover, the lines of causality are complex. This has been termed 'the vexatious fact of society': that 'we the people shape it, whilst it re-shapes us as we go about changing it or maintaining it, individually and collectively' (Archer 2007c: 38).

We need to also note that structure and agency are 'radically different things' (Bhaskar 1989: 76). Archer explains this by noting that 'an educational system can be centralized, while a person cannot, and humans are emotional, which cannot be the case for structures' (Archer 2010: 275). A further distinct difference is that structure and agency operate over different time periods. Structures can be relatively enduring while the life of the individual agent is limited. Moreover, as is so often noted, we are all born into circumstances not of our choosing. Thus, necessarily, structures predate the actions of individuals, and necessarily also, they postdate these actions (even if modified through those actions).

Using social theory that explores the interrelationship between structure and agency is a relatively new but promising direction for higher education research more generally, as signalled in the recent work by Ashwin (2008, 2009). He notes that failing to account for structure and agency has limited the explanatory potential of student learning research. He identifies two key limitations of work that focuses on 'approaches to learning'. First, because this work centres on students' perceptions of the learning environment, its explanatory frameworks are dominated by considerations of agency. Second, its characterisations of students tend to be as '"disembodied" learners', and thus it 'tends to underplay the importance of their identities and power relations in teaching and learning interactions'. Significantly, Ashwin notes that despite the massive changes in higher education since the 1970s when this theory was first developed, its basic explanatory framing has remained completely unchanged.

A recent article by Williams demonstrates the applicability of Archer's social realist theory to a study of student learning in higher education (Williams 2012). He links this to what has been considered an 'ontological turn' in student learning research, signalled through the recent work of higher education scholar, Ronald Barnett, arguing for a focus on students' 'being' and 'becoming' rather than just on knowledge and skills. Here it is important to caution against a simplistic interpretation of what this might mean: Williams notes rather pithily that 'Student centredness masquerades too easily as recognition of student agency . . .' (p. 300).

In his analysis Williams argues that we need to extract the notion of student learning from the 'vice-like linkage to teaching' (p. 301) that can be seen in so much of the literature. On this issue he employs a thoughtful observation from the anthropologist Jean Lave, who states:

> A close reading of research on how to improve learning shows that questions about learning are almost always met by educational researchers with investigations of teaching. This disastrous shortcut equates learning with teaching. . . . It deprives us at one and the same time of clear analyses of learners as subjects – and of teachers as subjects as well.
>
> (Lave 1996: 158)

Williams (2012: 320) argues that what is needed to underpin this work is an 'analytically and ontologically stronger basis for understanding the person who learns', and he demonstrates that Archer's theory is well suited to this task. By applying this approach to a particular case study in this book, it is hoped to further demonstrate its value for a wider audience of scholars.

In summary

The deliberations in this chapter began with a consideration of approaches that can broadly be characterised as empiricist, working towards objective and quantifiable observations of education. It is not so hard to find variables that might correlate with each other, whether you want to call these motivation or study orientation or academic success. Another model that is attractive is the medical model, where different teaching techniques are considered in the same way as different treatments to a clinical population.

Student learning research has critiqued these methods for ignoring the individual students with their particular experience of the educational environment – and thus we have seen the development of interpretive work that aims to characterise the individual student. Early work in this vein tended to be qualitative, but much quantitative work has also sought to develop models that relate the characteristics of the individual student to learning outcomes.

What all of this work misses is the possibility of accounting for both the effects of the individual student and the context in which they find themselves. Traditional approaches to education research have tended to privilege either structure or agency, and this is common in much social science work too – what Archer terms 'upwards conflation' (all about agency) or 'downwards conflation' (all about structure). An argument has been presented here that what is needed is a research approach that allows us to understand the interplay between these two. These are distinct and different entities, and it is only in a full characterisation of their interaction that we will be able to build any deep understanding of the place of student learning in higher education.

Furthermore, what is needed is not merely more variables – an explosion of variables has taken us precisely away from genuinely productive insights into education – but explanatory theory that can help us understand why we see the outcomes we do in education, and how we might change things to achieve different outcomes. To do this we need a sociologically informed take on the workings of structure – the distribution of resources and positions in society – and how this interacts with agency – the space for individual action. The following chapters will move in detail through a framework that will allow us to do precisely this.

Part II

Building a theoretical framework

This book has started to point to the relative impoverishment of much of the current debate in higher education, typically relatively uninformed by social theory. The view has been introduced that a realist perspective on education and society offers great promise towards building a deeper understanding of the social dynamics that underpin observed outcomes in education. In this Part the basic tools of a social realist approach to researching student learning are introduced. Chapter 3 focuses on critical realism as a broad ontological and methodological framing for social research. Chapter 4 outlines Archer's particular approach to realist social theory, the morphogenetic approach. Chapter 5 outlines Bernstein's pedagogic device in order to understand the workings of curriculum and pedagogy. Chapter 6 pulls in further concepts from Archer in order to build a perspective on student learning as the morphogenesis of agency. Throughout this theoretically focused section, key concepts are illustrated by their application to the context of engineering education.

Chapter 3

Critical realism as philosophical foundation

Critical realism is a philosophical position that provides the underpinnings for social realist theory and research. This chapter offers an outline of the basic tenets of critical realism.

A critical realist ontology

The foundational ontological claim of critical realism is that there is a reality independent from human experience. As humans we are able to create knowledge about this independently existing realm. But we need to take care not to conflate our knowledge of reality, and reality itself. In distinguishing between these two realms, critical realism notes that the reality of independently existing objects is intransitive – relatively enduring – while the realm of knowledge created by humans is transitive – temporal, open to change. To conceptualise the links between these realms critical realism puts forward the idea of a *stratified* ontology, consisting of distinct layers, or strata. Thus conceptualised, the world can be seen to comprise the observable parts (both the objective world of events, termed the *actual*, and the subjective perceptions of individuals, termed by critical realists the *empirical*) and that which we cannot observe but comprises the mechanisms that give rise to what we observe: the *real* (Bhaskar 1975). Here we need to note that, because the empirical domain is made up of our experiences, this means that it must be related to something that took place in the domain of the actual, and thus also causally originated in the domain of the real. This is what is termed a *depth ontology* and is represented in Table 3.1.

Critical realism is a philosophical perspective that has arisen in response to the limitations of much contemporary social science, and offers us a way to

Table 3.1 Critical realist ontology

Level	Referring to
Empirical	Subjective experiences
Actual	Objective observations
Real	Mechanisms that underpin actual observations and empirical experiences

significantly move forward in how we can think about education in context. Brad Shipway (2011), a young Australian scholar who has been exploring the application of critical realism to education research, notes that there has been an increased uptake of critical realism in education scholarship since the turn of the recent millennium. Contemporary critical realism was and continues to be largely developed by the philosopher Bhaskar, but remains a relatively 'broad church'. This can be especially noted in the discussions on what, exactly, is signalled by the 'critical' in 'critical realism' – largely there is agreement that this signals a similarly emancipatory commitment as in critical theory, but there are a range of other interpretations (Danermark 2002). Shipway writes:

> To utter the word 'critical' as well as the word 'realism' is not so much to mark out an area of publicly recognisable, clearly articulated debate as to issue an invitation to wide-ranging argument.
>
> (Shipway 2011: 6–7)

One key attraction of a realist approach, especially for education researchers who are located in science or engineering disciplines, is that the full philosophical package offers a way of thinking about knowledge generation in both the natural and the social worlds. Bhaskar (1998) helps us realise that although there are distinct ontological differences between these worlds, there are still overarching approaches to thinking about them that can productively run in parallel. What does it mean to regard the social world as 'real'? It is important to emphasise that as much as we recognise the social world as constructed, this does not necessarily mean that it is not real. In fact, it has been argued by some that social realism is a necessary corollary to social constructivism (Collins 2000).

Some scholars (for example, Crotty 1998) have argued that the realm of ontology is something best left to philosophers and need not concern the practical social scientist. For engineering educators especially there might be a wish to simply 'get on' with the research. Realist scholars point out the risks of this approach. When we assume that the way things are is the way they seem to be to us, we are committing what they term the 'epistemic fallacy'. We become limited by our own subjective worlds. Archer writes:

> Realism can never endorse the 'epistemic fallacy' and, in this connection, it must necessarily insist that how the world is has a regulatory effect upon what we make of it and, in turn, what it makes of us. These effects are independent of our full discursive penetration, just as gravity influenced us, and the projects we could entertain, long before we conceptualized it.
>
> (Archer 2007b: 12)

Furthermore, she also notes:

> Every social theorist or investigator has a social ontology. This may be quite implicit but it is also unavoidable because we can say nothing without making some assumptions about the nature of social reality examined.
>
> (Archer 2008: 464)

With critical realism, the objective of research is to develop explanations of observed and experienced phenomena that point to causal relations at the level of that which cannot be observed, the level of the real. The Australian social realist, Leesa Wheelahan, emphasises that this ontological position means that 'the world is not reducible to what we experience or what happens, there is much that could happen and understanding this is necessary if we are to think the unthinkable and the not-yet-thought' (Wheelahan 2009: 230). A realist explanation is thus, obviously, not only a description, but also not only an explanation of what happened. It also needs to encompass what could have happened, and what could not have happened.

Crucially, that the critical realist imputes mechanisms at the level of the real does not imply a mechanistic model of society. Structures cannot cause people to do things; the causal effects of structures are always mediated by human agency. Structures do make certain choices more attractive and maybe more feasible to the individual, and in that sense in which they condition agency they are causal. This causality is only activated in the context of the agent and their potential actions. Sayer describes it thus:

> A crucial implication of this ontology is the recognition of the possibility that powers may exist unexercised, and hence that what has happened or been known to have happened does not exhaust what could happen or have happened.
>
> (Sayer 2000: 12)

Emergence

A further aspect to the critical realist ontology – and highly significant for grasping its particular take on causality – is the notion of *emergence*, where two or more objects can give rise to a new phenomenon that cannot be reduced to the properties of the original objects. Neither can the emergent object be explained simply by references to the properties of its precursors. In the context of learning, we know that neural networks are physiologically needed for the acquisition of new knowledge, but to reduce learning to a physiological process is to misrepresent its full complexity. Here we can see that the stratified reality posited by the critical realists comprises not only the three layers of empirical, actual and real, but also that within these strata there are further layers. Collier (1998) offers an illustration by noting that everything is governed by the laws of physics; some, but not all, things are governed by biology; and a further subset of things are governed by capitalist economics. With regard to the social world, a relationship between two people can now be understood as an emergent good from the interaction between two people. Moving to the focus of the present book and the discussion in Chapter 1, we can now characterise the 'public good' outcomes of higher education as emergent from the complex system of interactions centred on knowledge that takes place in the university.

With regard to the 'major' strata in the critical realist ontology we need to note that, because of emergence, what we observe in the domains of the actual and the empirical cannot be simply reduced directly to mechanisms in the real; there is no linear relationship between cause and effect. Thus there is no possibility of a predictive social science, but there is a requirement to build explanatory theory that offers complex accounts of a stratified reality with chains of emergent causality.

A key point here is that what is posited is analytical, not philosophical, dualism. Structures only emerge from the activities of people, and it is merely an analytical move to separate the workings of structure and agency. Structures also only exert effects when they bump up against the intentions of human agents. They are always relational and emergent. But because they are emergent from human intentions they also cannot be reduced to human intentions; furthermore they cannot be equated with individual human intentions.

Developing realist explanatory theory

It is important to note here that for the critical realist, a statistical relationship between two variables is not an explanation at all, as emphasised by Bob Carter and Caroline New in the introduction to their edited collection (2004: 9). Although uncovering such a relationship might be the start of a process, it cannot be considered an end in itself. For a realist explanation one needs to develop abstractions that interrelate properties that are causally significant. Often the 'common-sense' variables that are used in research are actually what Sayer calls *chaotic conceptions* (after Marx) in that they are really a bundling together of dissimilar phenomena. A realist explanation requires the analytical disaggregation of causal properties. A useful example is provided by Carter and New in the context of a study that might use social class as a variable, measured simply by income or house ownership. The problem here is that social class is an emergent property and needs to be located within a broader explanatory theory for a study of this sort to make any real sense. A realist study would ask 'What must the world be like?' for social class to have the outcomes that are observed. Sayer notes:

> There is more to the world, then, than patterns of events. It has ontological depth: events arise from the workings of mechanisms which derive from the structure of objects, and they take place within geo-historical contexts. This contrasts with approaches which treat the world as if it were no more than patterns of events, to be registered by recording punctiform data regarding 'variables' and looking for regularities among them.
>
> (Sayer 2000: 15)

Here we have characterised a realist perspective on the old structure–agency debate: an approach that treats structure and agency as independently possessing properties and powers that influence each other. Both the highly deterministic structuralist view, which puts all causal power on structure, and the purely agential voluntarist view are not adequate to the task. It is worth noting again the temporal dimension to this view of reality: social structures always predate us; once again we are not born into a world of our own making or choosing. Similarly we need to remember that structures are relatively enduring, compared to the fleeting time scale of human interactions.

Engaging with critical realism is an invitation to take the knowledge that we already have about student learning in higher education and to reinterpret it in realist terms. Although there will be great benefit in research projects that are explicitly designed up front with a realist methodology, Carter and New note that 'what knowledge we do have can best be understood in realist terms, even if the method used to acquire it was not self-consciously realist' (Carter & New 2004: 1). In terms of the kind of knowledge that we need to consider, these scholars note that interpretive methods are always going to be an important part of the picture. Here they draw on Sayer, who states unequivocally: 'Meaning has to be understood, it cannot be measured or counted, and hence there is always an interpretive or hermeneutic element in social science' (Sayer 2000: 17). Importantly, though, the realist goes beyond the interpretive method to develop a causal explanation. The person's actions and meanings need to be located within the social settings where they find themselves and the logical set of constraints and enablements that confront them. Shipway notes that the first step in realist education research will thus be to 'seek the reasons and accounts of the agents who are involved in the situation under examination', but that these are not taken at 'face value' and thus need to be considered alongside data from other sources in order to build explanatory theory resting on an identification of mechanisms at the level of the real (Shipway 2011: 165). For the critical realist, reasons are real in that they have causal effects, but it is always noted that the stated reason that a person may give for some action may not be the 'real' reason; that will need to be sifted out from a careful analysis of data.

In summary

In education, critical realism notes that structures are real; they have an independent existence from the agents whose actions they constrain. Shipway describes the contribution of critical realism thus: 'When the reality of social structures is combined with the concept of *explanatory critique*, critical realism is able to reveal problems involved in the underlying structures and mechanisms of educational systems' (Shipway 2011: 161). He argues further for the significance of a certain degree of 'healthy scepticism' if we are to do the necessary critical interrogation of things that are currently taken for granted. The 'critical' in critical realism thus functions at two levels: as an injunction to look beyond the taken-for-granted, but also, with a nod to critical theory, with an orientation towards an emancipatory project for all in society.

Critical realism has offered a depth ontology that can assist in teasing out the different causal properties that are at play in the social world. A phenomenon of central significance is that of emergence, in which properties at one stratum combine to form an entity at another stratum that has properties that are not merely the sum of its components. Building realist explanatory theory involves an identification of such chains of emergent causality.

Now that we have located social research within the broader philosophical framework of critical realism, we turn to consider the particular social realist theory that will be adopted through this book, that of the sociologist Archer.

Chapter 4

Realist social theory
Archer's morphogenetic approach

Archer has a very distinctive social theory, termed the morphogenetic approach. It centres on structure, culture and agency, and this chapter proceeds to lay this framework out in some detail.

Structure, culture and agency

Archer has described the morphogenetic approach as a 'framework . . . of practical use to those working on substantive sociological problems' (Archer 2007c: 39). To begin to understand this approach we need to grapple with the distinctive meanings that Archer attaches to structure and culture, key social mechanisms operating at the level of the real in order to condition the possibilities for human agency, as summarised in Table 4.1.

As outlined above, the object of social realist research is to develop explanations of observed and experienced phenomena that point to causal relations at the level of that which cannot be observed. A considerable amount of sociological work to date has focused here on the workings of 'structure', and the way in which structure interrelates to the realm of human agency. The distinctive contribution of Archer has been to show that culture, the world of ideas, can be analysed in an analogous manner, and that the interrelations of culture with agency cannot be ignored. *Structure* (social structure) has to do with the matter of 'who has got the goodies', which can be material resources as well as positions within organisational structures. If we consider engineering education, which formally entered the academy only in the nineteenth century, we can see that the move from the shop floor to the university was a tremendous gain in structural advantage. Structural location within the university assures all the material benefits that come

Table 4.1 Structure and culture

Domain	Conditioning	Influencing
Structure	Social structure – resources, roles	Social interaction
Culture	Cultural system – logically interrelated propositions	Socio-cultural interaction

along with that: a supply of students wanting university degrees, funding (even if less than desired) for teaching them, and the societal legitimation that the status of a university programme offers. Interaction such as this that is conditioned by structure is termed *social interaction* by Archer.

In Archer's theory the term *culture* has a very specific meaning, which differs from how it is used, say, in anthropology, and certainly from its everyday usage. Archer's construct of culture can be roughly equated to Karl Popper's 'World 3' (Archer 1996: xvii), the world of ideas. The world of ideas comprises everything that could be comprehended by a human mind, and is described by Archer as the contents of all the libraries that have ever existed in the world. A subset of this realm, termed the *cultural system*, is the world of propositions, defined as 'that sub-set of items to which the law of contradiction can be applied' (Archer 1996: xviii). At the level of the real, of causal mechanisms, the culture–agency analysis focuses on the cultural system. At the level of interaction, however, what is pertinent is not so much the logical relationship between ideas, but the matter of who holds them and the degree to which others can be persuaded to take on these ideas, the world of *socio-cultural interaction*. Archer describes this aspect of culture as follows:

> Obviously we do not live by propositions alone (any more than we live logically); in addition, we generate myths, are moved by mysteries, become rich in symbolics and ruthless in manipulating hidden persuaders.
>
> (Archer 1996: xviii–xix)

Thus the full set of cultural properties includes what Archer terms the 'theoretical' and 'doctrinal' (Archer 2003: 135), but these operate at different levels. In analysing the cultural conditioning of the space that is engineering education, it can be seen that its structural location in the academy comes with a particular set of ideas on what is legitimate knowledge for a university degree. In its allying with the world of science, engineering came to create and valorise engineering science knowledge. What has been noted as 'academic drift' in engineering curricula is the outcome of a powerful set of cultural ideas, operating to condition the space for human interaction and giving rise to a large deal of causal consensus among the agents who operate in the space of engineering education.

Situational logics: complementarities and contradictions

Structure and culture work together to condition the environment that human agents will enter. To analyse structural and cultural conditioning we need to analyse the *situational logics* that are in place. A key distinction is in whether these relations are *necessary* (for example, in the roles of student and teacher – you cannot have one without the other) or *contingent* (accidental). Crucially, we need to look out for configurations where one can identify a high degree of system integration (coherence) in the structural and cultural systems; in these situational logics of *complementarities (compatibilities)* one can expect morphostasis where these are necessary relations. Contingent complementarities allow for some degree of system stability, but there is also some degree of elaboration to be expected. When we identify a low degree of system integration we can expect these situational logics of *contradiction* or *incompatibility* to predispose the system towards morphogenesis.

In the realm of structure – given in full in Table 4.2 – the key distinction is between a situation of complementarity (compatibility) versus one of incompatibility – describing whether groups have mutually reinforcing vested (material) interests or not. Necessary complementarities are the situational logics at the heart of morphostatic cycles; here we have mutually reinforcing positions that simply reproduce the status quo. Contingent complementarities are interesting because, while they support each other, they do also open up further opportunities. Incompatibilities, if necessary, lead to compromise, where both parties might need to lose something in order to maintain stability. Contingent compatibilities are situational logics where there is no need for the opposition to be maintained; this is all-out war and one party stands to lose.

In the realm of culture – given in full in Table 4.3 – an incompatibility can be described in terms of the clashing logic that is at the heart of this configuration: a contradiction. The situational logics follow an analogous pattern to those in the realm of structure except that the dynamics revolve around ideas instead of material positions and resources. In thinking about student learning in higher education, particularly in the context of a student body from diverse backgrounds, Williams (2012: 308) suggests this could be a particularly productive analytical move, 'to examine the cultural situational logics facing a student'. At the

Table 4.2 Situational logics in the domain of structure (after Archer 1995: 218)

Configuration of structural interests	Situational logic
Necessary complementarities (compatibilities)	Protection: mutually reinforcing relations
Necessary incompatibilities	Compromise: everyone makes some gains and losses
Contingent incompatibilities	Elimination: there is a loser
Contingent compatibilities	Opportunism: new opportunities for advancement

Table 4.3 Analogous situational logics in the domain of culture

Configuration of cultural interests	Situational logic
Concomitant (necessary) complementarities	Protection: mutually reinforcing ideas
Constraining (necessary) contradictions	Correction: modification of ideas
Competitive (contingent) contradictions	Elimination: one set of ideas is eliminated
Contingent complementarities	Opportunity: new opportunities for 'cultural free play'

simplest level this confirms what we already know about student learning; that for any growth to take place there needs to a conflict moving the student out of a 'comfort zone'.

To illustrate these concepts further we can consider the situational logics produced by the configurations of both culture and structure in the field of engineering education. Structurally we have noted that engineering education finds itself located within the academy but with strong links to the professional world. This is a structural situation of necessary complementarities that carries within it the potential for constraining contradictions over competing ideas, for example, when a university-accredited programme does not succeed in acquiring professional accreditation, as does occasionally happen, exposing different views on what required for accreditation. A further powerful structural consideration that plays out in this complex structural relation concerns economic resources: in the ongoing relative underfunding of higher education, the strong links that engineering education has with the industrial world are significant – a situation of deep necessary complementarity. These are effected through industrial bursary arrangements in South Africa and some other countries where students are funded to do engineering degrees in exchange for an employment commitment on graduation. Further economic support to engineering programmes accrues through industrial funding of research and in some cases even direct support of the undergraduate teaching endeavour, for example in the corporate funding of laboratories and teaching venues. Structurally, it might then seem that engineering education is located to get the best of both worlds: the status and legitimacy of the university and the material benefits of the capitalist world of work. These material relations may appear to be beneficial to both parties, but it is in the world of culture where clashes can emerge.

The cultural space associated with the profession has a slightly different way of valuing what should be in an engineering degree; here the judgement is on whether the graduate is 'ready for work'. The debates on the engineering degree across the twentieth century can be seen as a contestation between these different cultural ideas: between the world of knowledge (for its own sake, exemplified by science) and between the world of work (with its instrumental purposes). In the early decades situational logics of (necessary) contradiction prevailed, which issued a diversity of curriculum models on offer and frequent changes between these at particular institutions. In the post-war period onwards an accommodation of sorts – a situation of compromise – has come to bear, partly through a realigning of the purposes of university education in a more instrumental direction as degrees are argued as good for the economic advancement both of the individual and of society. Another aspect of this accommodation is that the professional accreditations have tended to be rather vague on specifics, leaving much of the actual content of the degree up to the university academics. That the clash between these two cultural spaces is not fully resolved can be noted in the ongoing debates over the purposes and form of the engineering degree.

It has been argued here that over time the contradictions that exist between the cultural space of the academy and that of the profession have been progressively accommodated, quite likely as a consequence of the structural arrangements that have evolved over time: it suits the profession to have engineers educated in the academy, and it suits the academy to have a profession that readily employs its graduates. The academy requires the legitimisation of engineering science, and the profession has learnt to tolerate the disjoint that exists between graduate skills and workplace skills.

The morphogenetic cycle

Thus, when Sizwe and his classmates embark upon a chemical engineering degree at the University of Cape Town, they enter a world that has been structurally and culturally conditioned by a complex set of prior interactions. Moreover, when a professor at that same university sets out to lecture a course, they are also entering a world of enablements and constraints. Archer stresses that this is the first stage of the morphogenetic cycle in which the situation that agents will involuntarily confront has been objectively shaped by both structural and cultural properties.

What happens next? At the heart of Archer's morphogenetic framework are the interactions that take place between agents in the social space. In the context of engineering education these are the interactions between students and lecturers, between students and other students, and between lecturers and other lecturers. Archer distinguishes analytically between those interactions that are structurally conditioned because of different positions and resources that the agents involved possess (termed social interactions), and those that are culturally conditioned because of the ideas (including knowledge) that are held by those concerned (termed socio-cultural interactions). Of course, this is only an analytical distinction, and in any observation of interaction these dimensions are heavily intertwined, but crucially we need to be able to pull apart the different influences of structure and culture if we are to produce a full Archerian analysis.

Thus we can expect that in the realm of structural properties we might note causal influences at play in, say, for example, a context where a student from a working-class background enters a university engineering programme that is structured on the presumption that students will have the material resources on hand, for example, to buy textbooks and to print out reports. The degree of causal influence of this structural conditioning will depend at least in part on whether this structural situation is supported by the cultural conditioning of the environment in terms of whether there is a strong set of ideas embodied by lecturers that assume that students need to have a particular background in order to succeed in engineering, or whether there is a cultural view at play that focuses on assisting all students to surmount the hurdles of succeeding in the degree.

We can also note here the useful analyses of 'engineering education culture' showing how in many parts of the world it has historically operated as a space where women generally feel less comfortable than men (Godfrey & Parker 2010).

These doctrinal ideas need to be analytically distinguished from the propositional world of engineering knowledge, but we do need to consider the degree of coherence between them. In other words, to what extent are the knowledge structures in engineering related to a particular social order that includes some groups and excludes others? In examining the interplay between structure and culture we do always, though, need to note the potential independence of these domains. Archer notes:

> Certainly some material relations may and frequently are legitimated by reference to ideas, but the two should not be elided, for a material relationship can be sustained by coercion and manipulation, thus its legitimation is not a matter of necessity.
>
> (Archer 1995: 175)

Crucially, though, at the level of interaction there are also independent causal relationships between groups and individuals. We know that individuals are able to work out for themselves courses of action within both the cultural and structural constraints they encounter, as seen so powerfully in the narrative of Sizwe. Importantly, the outcome of this stage is further elaboration of both structure and culture, thus forming the conditioning for further cycles of morphogenesis or morphostasis. Archer then goes on to show how changes in the realm of structure can impact on relations in the realm of culture, and vice versa. Morphostasis (reproduction of the existing order) or morphogenesis (transformation) can occur quite independently in the structural and cultural arenas, although change in one arena has the causal power to condition possibilities for change in the other arena. This is represented in Figure 4.1.

Crucially, then, we see that structure and culture come together during interaction; they 'intersect in the middle element of their respective morphogenetic cycles' (Archer 1996: xxviii). How does this happen? An interest group defending structural relations will endorse a set of ideas that may seem to advance its

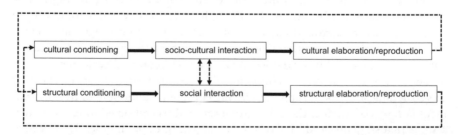

Figure 4.1 Intersection of morphogenetic cycles in structural and cultural domains (after Archer 2000: 271, 277)

Notes
The solid arrows indicate the trajectories of the basic morphogenetic cycles
The dotted arrows indicate possible interconnections between structural and cultural cycles

interests, but this then gets it embroiled in wider situational logics in the domain of culture. For those defending the position of engineering education in the academy, it has been shown that the support of industry and the associated arguments about the significance of engineering graduates for the economy has been very useful over time, but not completely unproblematic in terms of agreement about what should be in the curriculum. Similarly, one might have an interest group promoting a certain set of ideas but then finding themselves enmeshed in the constraints and enablements of the structural arrangements at play. Many academics still hold to an ideal of collegiality, but this is increasingly challenged by changing structural arrangements in the management of the university that put the university managers in a more corporate type of role. This intersection between cycles of structural and cultural morphogenesis is referred to by Archer as the 'interpenetration' between structure and culture (Archer 1996: xxviii).

In summary

We now have a well-kitted toolbox for doing a social realist analysis, with a core focus on the interactions of structure, culture and agency. Crucially we need to focus on the situational logics at play in a particular social context in order to examine the possibilities for morphogenesis or morphostasis. But the causality is complex: as much as structural and cultural conditioning does constrain and/or enable possibilities, in the world of human interaction it is sometimes possible for these constraints to be mediated.

With a focus on higher education, knowledge is central, experienced by students through the emergent structure of the curriculum. We thus need to build an extra set of theoretical tools that can help us grapple with the specificities of this aspect of reality, and we turn now to a social realist perspective on knowledge and curriculum.

Chapter 5

A social realist perspective on knowledge and curriculum

Knowledge is at the heart of any discussion on universities and student learning. What does it mean to have a *realist* perspective on knowledge? This chapter starts with addressing that question, then brings in a framework from the sociologist of education, Bernstein, that shows the connections between knowledge, curriculum and pedagogy.

A realist perspective on knowledge

A realist perspective grants a distinct ontological reality to knowledge, separate from the people who have generated it or even who hold it. Archer's model of cultural morphogenesis has already made this explicit, where she draws a sharp distinction between the cultural system and the ontological stratum that it inhabits, and the level of socio-cultural interaction where human interactions work to use and shape ideas in particular ways, resulting potentially in structural and/or cultural elaboration. This is of course to recognise, centrally, the *emergent* nature of knowledge.

Recent work by Moore (2009) sets out clearly the core tenets of a realist perspective on knowledge, which has a long history in the philosophy of science, building on a Kantian commitment with famous twentieth-century exponents being Karl Popper (see Popper 1966) and Rom Harré (see Harré et al. 1994). Moore notes how other – non-realist – philosophical perspectives have been influential to date in the sociology of education. Because scholars have focused on how knowledge is constructed in a social context it has been tempting to reduce it to that socio-cultural interaction, as is done in constructionist or relativist views, which do not distinguish between the knowledge and groups that hold it. These perspectives thus deny the possibility that knowledge can be 'based in anything other than the standpoints of those producing the knowledge and entwined with their particular social interests' (Moore 2009: 7). It is important here to note that this is also distinctly different from the positivist position, which assumes that knowledge can be entirely detached from its social context by 'grounding it in unmediated sense-data organized by propositional logic' (Moore 2009: 5). Constructionism set itself up in opposition to positivism and more generally to a naïve empiricism, but a realist perspective also rejects the ontological claims of constructionism. Signally, Moore demonstrates how constructionism and positivism both share an 'absence of ontology' when it comes to knowledge – 'issues of knowledge are, for both, reduced to an epistemology of the knowledge subject' (p. 10). However, where social realism does connect with constructionism is in its value commitments, in its desire for a more equitable society – here Moore argues that social realism has more potential to complete this project, because of its strong theory of knowledge (p. 15).

Furthermore, for something to be real it must have causal powers – we know this is so for knowledge because to hold a particular idea is to place oneself in a particular context of constraints and enablements. Thus we can talk about 'powerful knowledge', and we can also compare different knowledges as to their power. Here, we note that the kind of knowledge that is able to be abstracted from its context has a power in that it can be used in other contexts. This is the distinct power of scientific knowledge. A crucial contribution of a social realist approach to knowledge is the recognition that although dominant groups in society might have easier access to powerful knowledge, the solution going forward is not to try to valorise some other knowledges by virtue of their being held by dominant groups but rather to find ways to open up access for all groups to powerful knowledge. Crucially, a social realist view rejects the claim that because a certain form of knowledge is privileged, that this implies the privileging of 'a particular type of knower' (Moore 2009: 6). This is a key departure point of the present book. This does not mean an uncritical approach to knowledge; on the contrary, powerful knowledge is precisely that because it is open to ongoing critique. This 'strong model of knowledge' does not imply a defence of the canon based on absolutism. On the contrary, 'openness to the possibility of being judged wrong is more important than the ways in which we might claim to be right' (p. 14). Furthermore, it is also to recognise that various standpoint critiques have certainly in and of themselves generated useful data and new insights, but it is in their impoverished theories of knowledge that they are limited.

Knowledge therefore has an obvious and non-arbitrary, causal, relation to its object but, importantly, also a relation its subject, to the 'knower'. The properties of the object constrain the knowledge, but the properties of the subject, the 'knower', do not necessarily have to do so. These have been termed by Sayer and others 'epistemic' and 'social' relations respectively (Sayer 1992).

The field of production: the generation of knowledge

In an exploration of how knowledge is generated, in what he termed the *field of production*, Bernstein distinguished between *hierarchical* and *horizontal knowledge structures*. Hierarchical knowledge structures, as exemplified by science, grow knowledge vertically by subsuming new knowledge into existing knowledge. Horizontal knowledge structures, on the other hand, grow by adding new 'languages', which do not necessarily relate to existing knowledge. The sociologist Karl Maton, in a significant elaboration of this work, has argued that knowledge, always, has not only a *knowledge structure* but also what he terms a *knower structure*; here the knower structure defines the strength of the social relation, describing whether a significant part of the knowledge-generation process is the cultivation of the 'right sort' of knower. At the heart of this distinction is the question of what is the 'principal motivation' in the field (Maton 2010): is it developing knowledge (as in science, where creating specialised knowers is a means to this end) or is it developing knowers (where creating specialist knowledge is a means to this end)?

A further key concept in this regard is that of *grammaticality*. The 'grammar' of a knowledge structure refers to 'the degree to which its concepts and relations can be operationalized to provide relatively precise and consistent empirical descriptions that allow the knowledge to be tested and confirmed or disconfirmed empirically' (Luckett 2010: 14). This is essentially describing the strength of the epistemic relation. Hierarchical knowledge structures tend to display relatively strong grammars, compared to horizontal knowledge structures.

Knowledge is indeed socially constructed. Powerful knowledge tends to be constructed in communities that have systematic modes for its production, the disciplines. Things are arranged in these communities so that the epistemic relation is stronger than the social relation. Moore (2012) notes that these communities operate in 'relatively autonomous modes', with their own 'logics and capacities', and thus the generation of knowledge cannot simply be equated with individual experience (p. 13). Knowledge thus becomes located within 'networks that are extensive in time and space and relatively independent from any particular social (experiential) base' (p. 9). Disciplinary communities have methodologies for judging the validity of knowledge claims and for signifying new knowledge as legitimate knowledge. Thus, as noted by Luckett, 'all knowledge is fallible, but not equally so' (Luckett 2010). Here we are thus disaggregating Archer's cultural system, the full set of any intelligible ideas at a given time, into distinct subsets, which have close relationships (logical relations) with each other. Thus, from a realist perspective knowledge structures are primarily potentially enabling, rather than constraining of human agency, and actually operate as sites of production rather than just reproduction (Moore 2012).

The field of recontextualisation: the formation of curriculum

Within the university, a key activity is the transmission of knowledge from experts to novices, the central focus of this book: student learning. In this arena, the curriculum is the structure in which students encounter knowledge. The curriculum is the outcome of prior processes in which various power interests (not only academics) made a selection of disciplinary knowledge, and organised it into a particular sequence with associated milestones to signal achievement. The process whereby knowledge is translated from the field of production, where knowledge is generated, to the arena of curriculum, is termed by Bernstein *recontextualisation*. Two key modes of curricula are identified: the *collection code*, where there are sharp knowledge boundaries between the different components of the curriculum, and the *integrated code*, where boundaries between different components are not as marked. These two modes are 'ideal types' in the sense that they describe the parameters in which real curricula, which tend to be combinations of modes, exist.

Ashwin (2009) notes the distinctive space of higher education, where it is quite possible to find the same set of people engaged in generating knowledge, recontextualising it into curriculum, and teaching and assessing in courses. Schooling is marked by the confinement of school teachers to the last level above. The pedagogic device is a site of struggle. Inscribed on the curriculum are the past cycles of morphogenesis, the tussles between the interests of the academy and of other interested parties, for example, the state, the profession, and so on. As it now stands it represents a long morphostasis in this cultural space but remains a site for contestation.

Crucially, because curriculum knowledge is recontextualised disciplinary knowledge, its structure is not arbitrary. If its disciplinary knowledge base is one that rests on open questioning of knowledge claims, then a curriculum that is true to its origins has to carry forward these commitments. If a disciplinary base has a strong epistemic relation, one would expect to see the same orientation in the curriculum.

An important contribution of Bernstein's framework for analysing curriculum is the analytical construct of *classification*, which refers to the boundaries between categories of knowledge. It is in the legitimation of these boundaries that power is exerted (Bernstein, 2000). Ashwin notes that it is in classification that 'disciplinary knowledge practices maintain their specialized voices' (Ashwin 2009: 94). For example, traditional engineering curricula exhibit strong classification, especially at the lower levels involving exposure to a range of *singulars*, but the final-year design project – which attempts to prepare students for the real world of engineering practice, characterised by Bernstein as a *region* – involves a weakening of classification as students are expected to integrate engineering science knowledge from different areas, as well as incorporate engineering practice knowledge where appropriate (Kotta, 2008). Alongside classification Bernstein identifies *framing*, referring to matters such as selection of content, sequencing and pacing, as the key means whereby control is exercised, socialising individuals into particular identity spaces. From this perspective one can see that traditional engineering curricula that are largely prescribed and content-loaded tend to be strongly framed.

Knowledge boundaries are significant in the Bernsteinian analysis. Young and Muller state this clearly:

> By emphasising the social differentiation of both knowledge and institutions, social realist approaches challenge the widely shared assumption that boundaries are always barriers to be overcome rather than also conditions for innovation and the production and acquisition of new knowledge. As Bernstein (2000) argues, boundaries play an important role in creating learner identities and are thus the conditions for acquiring 'powerful knowledge' as well as being barriers to learning.
>
> (Young & Muller 2010: 16)

The field of reproduction: the arena of pedagogy

The next transformation is what happens when the formal curriculum becomes enacted in the classroom, the realm of pedagogic practice – termed by Bernstein the *field of reproduction*. It is important to note that this arena of pedagogy is the area where lecturers have the capacity to influence student access to knowledge. Pedagogic practice proceeds through *evaluative rules*, which are the criteria by which teachers judge whether students have produced 'legitimate text', that is, whether they can display their knowledge in ways that would be considered appropriate. Bernstein suggested two modes of pedagogic practice: *visible (or performance) pedagogies*, where there is strong classification and framing, and thus clear signalling to students of what is required of them; and *invisible (or competence) pedagogies*, where the assessment is more based on the individual student rather than objective performance in a test. Although it has been argued that much of higher education rests on visible pedagogies (Ashwin 2009), in the context of engineering education it can be argued that invisible pedagogies come to play where the regionality of the knowledge is more in evidence, such as in the design project.

The distinctiveness of engineering science and the transition from engineering science knowledge to design knowledge is starting to be explored by education researchers (Smit 2012a; Wolmarans *et al.* 2012). Design courses in traditional engineering curricula are introduced towards the senior years of the programme, and the final-year design project is often what constitutes the 'capstone' course and is a key determinant of overall success or failure in the programme. Here students move from mastering a particular part of engineering science in a dedicated theoretically focused course towards needing to integrate knowledge across engineering science as well as incorporating other modes of working including heuristics to tackle an open-ended problem, which is intended to model the kinds of design problems that are found in real-world engineering practice.

In the realm of pedagogy we are considering the ways in which teachers structure educational experiences in order to make learning possible. Once again, the non-arbitrary aspects of the disciplinary knowledge structure, as carried through into curriculum, also have implications for pedagogy. Muller (2006) notes that the more hierarchical a body of knowledge, the more likely it is that pedagogy will need strong sequencing, so that students will have the requisite prior knowledge for a new topic. Key concepts learnt at the lower levels need to be retained and built upon when engaging in more advanced courses. Maton (2009) describes this as cumulative learning, something long recognised of significance by scholars of science and mathematics education. What we also now know from a few decades of this research is the crucial importance of conceptual understanding. We know that students can certainly successfully mount assessment hurdles without actually understanding basic concepts in the course, given the formulaic nature of much assessment. However, in an engineering programme where second year builds on first year, third year builds on second year, and fourth year builds on third year, if one is missing a key point of understanding in the first year it can have devastating consequences when attempting to grasp more sophisticated concepts at the senior levels.

The strength of the social relation in the parent knowledge structure is also of significance here. For disciplines with strong social but weak epistemic relations (also termed 'knower code' disciplines), where the instantiation of the 'ideal knower' is paramount, there are particular challenges for pedagogy when students do not necessarily have the ideal 'cultivation' in their home and school backgrounds. In science and engineering, on the contrary, we should find that, because the social relation is less significant in the field of production, the cultural capital of the learner should matter less in the field of reproduction.

Drawing on Foucault, Bernstein used the metaphor of a *gaze* to describe the specialised consciousness that constitutes successful learning in a disciplinary area. He describes gaze as 'a particular mode of recognising and realising what counts as an "authentic" . . . . reality' (Bernstein 1999: 165). In an elaboration of this idea, Maton (2010) outlines a range of relevant forms of gaze in particular disciplinary areas, with the one polarity of the 'trained gaze' more likely in disciplines like science that have strong epistemic but weak social relations. Here the gaze involves learning to take on specialised procedures and methods. (On the other pole is the 'born gaze' in which you really need to be born into the right kind of family to be able to take on this gaze, such as in the traditional forms of the humanities.)

In short, in engineering – at least in engineering science – we have knowledge structures with very explicit and strong grammars, and thus anyone should be able to learn them, given the appropriate pedagogical cues. The caveat of course is that the 'anyone' needs to have had the appropriate prior knowledge built up in previous years of education, and this is too often lacking given the wide and often unsatisfactory range of schooling experiences out there.

In summary

The full model put forward here by Bernstein is termed the *pedagogic device* and is summarised in Table 5.1.

Table 5.1 The pedagogic device (after Maton & Muller 2007: 19)

Field	Definition	Ordered by
Production	The ordered regulation and distribution of a society's worthwhile store of knowledge	*Distribution rules*
Recontextualisation	The transformation of this store into a pedagogic discourse	*Recontextualising rules*
Reproduction	The further transformation of this pedagogic discourse into a set of evaluative criteria to be attained	*Evaluative rules*

For the purposes of this book and the questions that animate it we need to con-nect issues of knowledge and curriculum back to students and student learning. Luckett notes that 'curriculum practices construct particular identities and forms of agency for students'. She continues:

> Learning is not only about acquiring content and developing skills; it is also about becoming and transforming the self. In order to do this, a curricu-lum should take students beyond the limitations of their natal contexts and cultures. They should learn about powerful, decontextualized, abstract and specialized forms of knowledge. However, in order to engage in (national) development and contribute to society, they need to return to concrete con-texts of practice, and start seeing their old worlds in new, reflexive ways.
>
> (Luckett 2010: 19)

In the following chapter key ideas from Archer's conceptualisation of student agency are drawn upon in order to start to build an informed perspective on student learning.

Chapter 6

Conceptualising student agency

The central focus for this book is on the student and on student learning, the stated objective of higher education. It has been noted that the ways that student learning has been researched to date have their limitations, and the focus of this book is on developing new ways for researching student learning. If we take a critical realist perspective, using the sociology of Archer, how might we think about student learning? This chapter uses Archer's theory to build a stratified concept of student agency.

A stratified model of being human

A key starting point to critical realism is the notion of a stratified reality, and this means that we can also conceptualise the student in stratified terms. A flat ontology gives us one dimension for thinking about the person, while in a critical realist ontology we can conceptualise layers of *personal emergent properties*. Archer summarises it thus:

> In fact, the stratified view of humanity advocated here sees human beings as constituted by a variety of strata. Each stratum is emergent from, but irreducible to, lower levels because all strata possess their own *sui generis* properties and powers. Thus, schematically, mind is emergent from neurological matter, consciousness from mind, selfhood from consciousness, personal identity from selfhood, and social agency from personal identity.
>
> (Archer 2000: 87)

Personal identity

Underpinning a social realist take on human agency is the recognition that this is first of all founded on a *continuous sense of self*, something that is established very early on in child development and which is emergent from our embodied experience of the world. It does not depend on language or on culture. Archer (2007b: 12) quotes Mauss (1989: 3): 'there has never existed a human being who has not been aware, not only of his body but also of his individuality, both spiritual and physical.'

This is only the start. As they develop, humans 'become the bearers of further emergent properties and powers which are what make them recognisable as subjects who respond differently to the world and act within it to change it' (Archer 2007b: 15). The next step, temporally, is the emergence of *personal identity*, achieved through adolescence into young adulthood for most individuals. This captures what you care about, what matters to you, and in what you then decide to invest your time and energy. The emergence of personal identity is summarised in Figure 6.1.

Archer suggests that we encounter reality in three orders: the natural order, the practical order and the social order. The *natural order* relates to our bodily experience of the world and of our own bodies: being hungry, being cold, and so on. We share this experience with other animals, and these experiences are embodied in that they are not abstracted, they are direct. If you are tired and hungry, that is a material reality that has severe limitations on your ability, for example, to learn. What distinguishes us from animals is our tendency to develop what is termed a material culture, the world of artefacts, which we both develop and use towards our own ends. This aspect of the world is termed by Archer the *practical order*. The third order, which is also a distinctly human experience, is that of the *social order*, which encompasses propositional culture. Studying engineering involves acquiring knowledge that is predominantly in the social order since it is discursive and related to the cultural system. Although, for example, learning to write a computer program does ultimately relate to working with an artefact, it is mediated through the discursive world, in the same way that writing is much more than manipulating a pencil over paper.

Living simultaneously in these three orders, we experience concerns. The *internal conversation* is the space where we weigh up these different concerns and decide on a way forward. Archer stresses that evaluating and prioritising our concerns is an activity in which we use our emotions. Emotions are described as 'com-

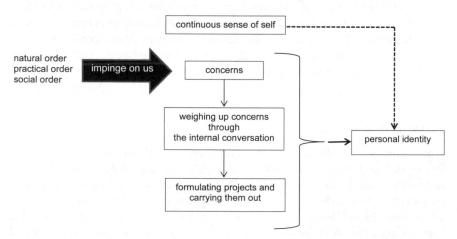

Figure 6.1 The emergence of personal identity

mentaries on our concerns'; emotionality is 'our reflexive response to the world' (Archer 2007b: 16). In a strong challenge to rational choice theory, Archer sees human decision-making as taking place through the weighing up of different emotional imports, rather than a purely rational exercise. In deciding what matters to us and in comparing the relative weight of different concerns we cannot avoid our emotions as a mode of engagement. Thus is signalled another crucial contribution of Archer's theory to a consideration of student learning: the possibility of fully accounting for the central role of the affective. Williams (2012) notes that recent findings in the field of cognitive neuroscience offer further support for these claims.

Our personal identity rests in how we undertake this internal conversation and in what we decide to care about, our 'constellation of concerns' (Archer 2007c: 40). Williams thus writes: 'When we make decisions about our concerns, we do so under our own descriptions: they are fallible choices, but they are our choices' (Williams 2012: 314).

What we care about and how we decide to proceed with regard to that is the formulation of a project. Humans typically are engaged in more than one project simultaneously, in fact to entirely neglect concerns in one order is to risk their well-being in the others. Archer writes that:

> . . . a dilemma now confronts all people. It arises because every person receives all three kinds of emotional commentaries on their concerns, originating from each of the orders of reality – natural, practical and social. Because they have to live and attempt to thrive in the three orders simultaneously, they must necessarily, in some way and to some degree, attend to all three clusters of commentaries. This is their problem.
>
> (Archer 2007b: 16)

In resolving this dilemma we achieve a *modus vivendi*, a way in which we will go about our being in the world. Here we need to manage a multitude of concerns, but we also need to disaggregate some sense of our *ultimate concerns*, the things that matter to us most and which are long-term objectives. Archer notes that the achievement of personal identity is usually timed in early adulthood. Some adults never achieve this, and possibly this explains part of the experience of the addict or the homeless person, who can never move beyond the satisfaction of immediate concerns.

Modes of reflexivity

In exploring the ways in which people conduct their internal conversations, a recent empirical study by Archer and her team (Archer 2007a) has uncovered distinctively different modes, which are termed modes of reflexivity, summarised in Figure 6.2. *Communicative reflexivity* involves making your decisions through discussions with others. Crucially, if your immediate community does not have

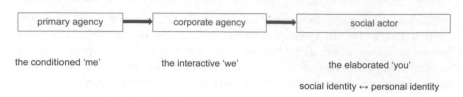

Figure 6.2 The emergence of personal and social identity (after Archer 2000: 296)

wide experience of higher education and you are using a communicative mode of reflexivity, you are unlikely then to choose to study. It is not so much that the prevalence of particular modes of reflexivity is linked to class (Archer finds no evidence for this), but that the communicative mode tends to link you to the aspirations and life experiences of your immediate others, and thus tends to be associated with staying in the structural circumstances of your birth context. If you have a class background where everyone goes on to higher education and you are a white male then the decision to study engineering might easily be made through a mode of communicative reflexivity.

There are two other modes of reflexivity that appear to be more associated with the choice to study; interestingly both of these involve some disjuncture with one's immediate social context. *Autonomous reflexives* hold their internal conversations without much need for outside consultation and formulate personal projects that involve achieving high levels of competence in their chosen skills. *Meta-reflexives* focus their internal conversations around social ideals and formulate projects in relation to their dissatisfaction with the social circumstances of others. Significantly, Archer's model does not suggest that an individual person will engage in only one mode of reflexivity in their life; she does, however, see that at particular stages in life a predominant mode of reflexivity can be identified.

Social identity

A social realist approach allows for a nuanced understanding of the role of society in constituting the individual. As opposed to the two polar extremes, which posit either the 'self-made man' who is unaffected by society, or the person who is fully determined by society, Archer inserts the person with all their personal emergent properties and powers into a structural and cultural context whose constraints they mediate and navigate. To account for our 'social selves', Archer introduces the concepts of *agent* and *actor*, which emerge from the impact of the structural and cultural context on ourselves and our personal identities. In a two-way relationship, the nascent *social identity* also acts backs on the personal identity. 'Social identity is the capacity to express what we care about in social roles that are appropriate for doing this' (Archer 2007b: 17).

Two types of agent are identified in the emergent development of social identity: the primary agent and the corporate agent. These emerge from the relation between the individual and the structural and cultural context in which they find themselves. Archer insists that these are both plural identities, which involve a connection in a broader group. *Primary agency* results from the circumstances of one's birth; each person involuntarily obtains a place in the distribution of society's resources. This involves becoming part of a group that is 'equally privileged or underprivileged' (Archer 2000: 261), and is something over which one has no choice. *Corporate agency* results from agents collectively joining together in an attempt to change society. Primary agency is a passive power while corporate agency is active. Both have the potential to effect structural and/or cultural morphogenesis – primary agency from sheer demographic numbers and corporate agency through coordinated action. In the South African context, Kathy Luckett notes that 'black students are typically portrayed as exercising only primary agency, i.e. they influence the situation only through the impact of their (increasing) numbers and high failure rates' (Luckett 2012: 342). Williams makes a related comment, noting that students' powers as primary agents are exerted simply as a 'stream of environmental pressures and problems', while the exertion of power through, for example, a student representative council or a student evaluation, can be considered as an instance of corporate agency (Williams 2012: 309).

From a historical perspective, Archer argues that contemporary times have allowed for a growing significance of corporate agency, with a proliferation of corporate groupings that are not necessarily closely linked to primary agency. She also argues that primary agency is shrinking in terms of its social significance. This is an important observation in the context of higher education, where the development of corporate agency among students from diverse backgrounds becomes increasingly possible.

Both primary and corporate agency are group identities; by contrast, the actor, termed here a *social actor*, is an individual achievement, a person who is able to 'personify' a social role in a distinct manner. This involves 'finding a role(s) in which they feel they can invest themselves, such that the accompanying social identity is expressive of who they are as persons in society' (Archer 2000: 261). Becoming a social actor is what Archer refers to as the full attainment of a social identity. Social identity can thus be described as 'the capacity to express what we care about in social roles that are appropriate for doing this' (Archer 2007b: 17). Importantly, it is personal identity that enables the individual to occupy and form a role in this distinct manner. At the same time, as mentioned above, we need to note the ways in which the emerging social identity works back on the personal identity. Williams describes it thus: '. . . we experiment with personifying the role, and reflexively evaluate by attending to the emotional commentary on our concerns, our experience' (Williams 2012: 316).

To achieve social identity involves a full dialectical relationship between personal and social identity, characterised by Williams as the point where 'we have to reflexively question how much of our selves we will invest in the role' (Williams 2012: 317). Crucially, we need to note that it not possible to fully achieve personal identity without a social identity, but also vice versa.

The morphogenesis of agency

Archer's (2007) full model for the morphogenesis of human agency can thus be summarised as follows. Temporally prior to interaction is the primary agent, the person who is born into a set of life collectivities – what Archer terms the 'conditioned "me"'. In the phase of human interaction we see the development of corporate agency, the 'interactive "we"'. The full outcome of agential morphogenesis is the synthesis of personal identity and social identity into the 'elaborated "you"', the emergence of the social actor. This is represented in Table 6.1.

What does this mean for student learning in higher education? If graduateness is to mean anything worthy of the enormous investment that is made by society, one should surely anticipate that full agential morphogenesis would be a desired outcome for higher education: the individual who has arrived at some degree of internal consensus about what matters to them, and who has invested their efforts into a programme and has gone through the tough business of acquiring disciplinary knowledge in order to build a social identity that is in concert with the emerging personal identity. Williams offers a pertinent quote from Packer and Goiceochea (2000: 235):

> . . . learning presumes a social context – but in addition, person and social world are in dynamic tension, and community membership sets the stage for an active search for identity, the result of which is that both person and community are transformed. Learning entails both personal and social transformation – in short, ontological change.

As a sociologist, Archer's key concerns are about the morphogenesis of structure and culture: how does society change and how can we explain this change? A somewhat secondary concern for the sociologist is the morphogenesis of agency, termed by Archer the *double morphogenesis* (Archer 1995: 190). With a focus on researching student learning in higher education we are actually centrally focused on student agency and the possibilities for the development of such agency.

The central means for the morphogenesis of agency in higher education is the acquisition of knowledge. Here we have the interplay between our human powers and the discursive world, and in acquiring knowledge we obtain identities that

Table 6.1 Modes of reflexivity

Mode	Involves
Communicative reflexivity	Externalising the internal conversation; getting approval from others
Autonomous reflexivity	Formulating your own plan in your own head, regardless of what those in natal context might say
Meta-reflexivity	Focusing on social ideals and formulating projects to improve the lives of others

are specialised. Knowledge in a realist sense has properties and powers, and, thus acquired, constrains and enables new courses of action for the human subject.

In summary

A key aspect of Archer's conceptualisation of human agency is that it comprises a stratified model of the human, starting with the most fundamental and earliest awareness, which is of a distinct self – a continuous sense of being the same person and being separate from the world around one. The next stage of human development is that of personal identity: a sense of what we care about. We start to develop this when we need to weigh up emotional imports from the different orders in the world: the natural world that grants us bodily sensations, the practical world in which we learn to use artefacts, and the social world in which we engage in discursive acts. In our internal conversation we learn to prioritise those aspects that we care about most.

At the same time, we have an emergent social identity. At birth we are endowed with a particular life chances, which characterise our primary agency. At some point in life we might start to work together with others towards particular ends; this is termed corporate agency. The final achievement in social identity is that of becoming a social actor, where we manage to embody a social role in a manner that allows full expression of our primary identity. With regard to higher education, at this point the suggestion is made that the achievement of becoming a social actor should surely be the desirable outcome for higher education: of a graduate who has developed sufficiently personally to have something to care about but who has also through an engagement with knowledge made themselves able to take on a social role that is in concert with their ultimate concerns.

This chapter has wrapped up the delivery of theoretical tools that we need to have in hand in order to do a social realist analysis of student learning in higher education, building on Archer's sociology, and drawing in concepts from the realist sociology of education, building particularly on work deriving from that of Bernstein. We are now ready to run through an exemplar analysis, focusing here on a case study conducted with chemical engineering students at the University of Cape Town.

Part III

Developing a case study in engineering education

In this part of the book the theoretical tools that have been outlined are now applied to a particular case study involving third-year chemical engineering students at the University of Cape Town. There are two respects in which this case study needs to be located: geographically within the context of South African higher education (Chapter 7) and disciplinarily within engineering education (Chapter 8). In both spheres we need to trace the historical antecedents that have led to the particular situational logics in which these students find themselves.

Once located, the study unfolds, in Chapters 9 through 13. Taking the temporal significance for morphogenesis, Chapter 9 concerns the choice to study engineering. This sets up students for a particular journey that they could never more than partly envisage. Chapters 10 to 12 consider a range of dimensions of the experience of studying engineering, and Chapter 13 draws the study together.

The study is strongly informed by a narrative methodology, and the format of a book has been used to give freer licence than is usual in the presentation and analysis of data. Thus, Chapter 9 starts with a only small number of narratives, and with each chapter additional narratives are incorporated, thus building the analysis incrementally. Across these chapters the stories of 14 students comprising Sizwe and some of his classmates are unpacked and sifted for meaning, working towards the development of explanatory theory that can help us understand *why* we see the learning patterns we do in this and other similar contexts in higher education. The format of the chapter, with the careful building of an analysis narrative by narrative, is a deliberate choice that attempts to demonstrate closely what a social realist analysis entails.

Chapter 7

Geographical context for the study

Locating UCT chemical engineering

Here the chemical engineering programme at the University of Cape Town is located within its national context, with historical antecedents and contemporary challenges.

Higher education in South Africa

The first universities in South Africa were established during the nineteenth century, and in that context largely catered to an elite of the white population. With the focus towards Afrikaner nationalism growing in the early part of the twentieth century, the establishment of what emerged as Afrikaans medium universities was a significant development. Black students were never explicitly a part of the vision in either of these sectors, although in very small numbers some did enrol at the English-medium universities. Following the advent of apartheid in 1948, these institutions were officially designated for whites only.[1] There was muted but limited protest at the English-medium universities, who largely, it has to be acknowledged, towed the apartheid line. The apartheid state, having excluded black students from these institutions, proceeded to establish universities for the different race groups. These latter institutions operated off a lower unit of resource and were heavily policed for dissident views. During the 1980s, with the relaxation of some apartheid laws, universities were opened to all who wished to enrol and who met the entrance criteria. Many black students now enrolled at the English-medium institutions; during the 1990s the Afrikaans-medium institutions also dramatically increased their enrolment of black students. The universities designed for black students by the apartheid state remained black and relatively under-resourced.

With the advent of a democratic government in South Africa in 1994, the state was faced with the massive task of reshaping this inherited higher education landscape. In the first decade of the present century, it proceeded via a programme of mergers, which affected most institutions except for some of the top tier of the formerly white universities.

At the time of writing, the national debate has largely shifted from issues of 'access' to 'success'. Although participation rates remain low – overall 16 per cent of the cohort are enrolled in higher education; disaggregated by race, this is 60 per cent of white youths compared to 12 per cent of black African youths – an influential study has shown the massive inefficiencies of the system even with this highly selective participation. Of the full cohort that entered universities in 2001, five years later only 38 per cent had graduated, while 45 per cent had dropped out without graduating (Scott et al. 2007).

A tragic event early in 2012 illustrated starkly the level of the challenge regarding higher education in South Africa (Habib 2012). The University of Johannesburg had 800 places still open in its programmes and, as has been their practice in the past, allowed for last-minute applications for these. A 3 km queue formed on the designated day, and, following some chaos in the crowd, a stampede ensued: a mother of an aspirant student was killed, and a number of others were injured. This event attracted huge media attention in South Africa and abroad. Local commentators pointed out that many school leavers in impoverished schools are not sure whether they will achieve the required marks for university entry, struggle to find even the nominal application fee, and thus do not submit applications during their final year at school. When the marks are released in early January, an opportunity then to gain access to a university for the year is highly attractive, especially in a national context where there is up to 70 per cent youth unemployment.

Schooling in contemporary South Africa

The contemporary schooling landscape in South Africa continues to bear the markers of its colonial and apartheid past (see, for example, Hill et al. 2012; Hunter 2010). A minority of schools are of a very high quality and achieve outcomes that are internationally comparable while the vast majority continue to suffer a legacy of dysfunctionality and low quality. During apartheid, state schooling was stratified along racial lines. The schools that were designated during this period for black African students are today largely still of a poor quality and still tend to enrol only black African students. In this book I use the designation 'township school' or 'rural school' to refer to these schools, since the urban (township) school context is somewhat different from the rural one (some of these rural schools produce relatively good school results), although both, in general, offer schooling of a relatively poor quality. Schools that were designated for Indian or coloured students today tend to enrol a mix of black students depending on the geographical context, and are of middling quality, although some historically Indian schools offer education of a very high calibre. Schools that during apartheid were designated for white students nowadays enrol a mixed cohort of students and are thus in general parlance referred to as 'multiracial (state) schools'. These multiracial schools are generally fee-paying (with possibilities for fee exemption depending on family income) and thus enrol a largely middle-class student body with a minority of fee-exempt pupils. With their historical legacy of quality and their contemporary ability to buy in extra teaching staff they largely continue to offer a high-quality school education. The private school sector in South Africa is growing as elsewhere in the world and exhibits much diversity here, from extremely expensive traditional private schools with a mixed but generally wealthy enrolment down to relatively low-fee schools (some of which are church schools) that cater largely to a black population who have an aspiration for schooling better than that of the (state) township schools.

Thus, education is a key issue on the national agenda. Notwithstanding a recognition of the limiting impact of a schooling system that largely continues to be characterised by low quality and general dysfunctionality, at least for the black majority, there is a recognition that universities cannot wait for the generations that are likely to be needed for this situation to be remedied. Academic development in South Africa is a field of study and development in which universities seek to do the very best they can do with their intakes of students (Boughey 2007). This case study emerges from this context of concerns.

The University of Cape Town

The University of Cape Town (UCT) is one of the long-established English-medium institutions mentioned above, and during apartheid was designated for white students only. It enjoys a high status nationally and continentally, and garners notable international recognition. It currently has a student enrolment of approximately 25,000, with just over two thirds of these registered for undergraduate qualifications. Over half of UCT's enrolments are black students, coming from across South Africa. Some 20 per cent of the enrolments are international students, largely from across the continent.[2]

The chemical engineering programme at UCT is one of the oldest in the country, established during the 1950s, and for some time produced the largest graduating class nationally. It enjoys strong links with industry both in its undergraduate and postgraduate programmes. Of the South African students in the undergraduate programme, many enjoy some industrial funding of their studies, usually in the form of bursaries, which involve a commitment to work for the company after graduation. During the 1980s, UCT spearheaded efforts in engineering to promote the success of black engineering students, and the student cohort has been majority black since the early 1990s, with white students typically comprising about a quarter of the class. A major concern centres on the success of students, with typically in the order of only 65 per cent of the incoming cohort obtaining the degree, and only about half of these managing this in the regular four years of the programme (Case 2012). Over nearly two decades a range of initiatives have been put in place to respond to this challenge, including curriculum reform, teaching reform and the establishment of two lecturing posts focusing on academic development, one of which I have occupied since 1996.

A particularly notable and longstanding academic development initiative of the then Faculty of Engineering at UCT was the establishment in the early 1980s of an academic support programme, a curricular innovation that offered an extended degree for students from educationally disadvantaged backgrounds. The ASPECT programme (Academic Support Programme for Engineering at Cape Town) continues to this day, and a recent study showed that it has produced the bulk of the Faculty's black engineering graduates during the period between 1988 and 2003 (Kloot 2011). Sizwe, whose narrative opened this book, as well as many of his classmates, had entered UCT chemical engineering through the ASPECT programme.

The case study that features in this part of the book is derived from a study that was carried out with UCT students in a third-year chemical engineering course, termed here 'advanced reactor engineering'. Although a fairly conventional theoretically oriented course with lectures, afternoon problem-solving sessions (termed tutorials), a class test and a final examination, there were many elements of the course that were innovative and aimed towards supporting student learning and the development of conceptual understanding. For example, over the duration of the course students engaged in a design project, which required them to apply the course concepts to a complex real-world problem. This project entailed significant class discussion, group work and many interactions with the lecturer as the course progressed. Although the students perceived this as a relatively challenging course, they were especially positive about their experiences of the lecturer and the course. This seemed, however, at odds with the final course results, in which a quarter of the class failed, and less than a third achieved a final mark of more than 60 per cent.

The study aimed to characterise students' experiences of the course and to understand the apparent disjuncture between students' positive descriptions of the course and their poor course results. Being on sabbatical that semester, and not having previously completed a similar course in my own undergraduate studies, I decided to enrol in the course as a participant observer in order to provide contextual background for an exploration of student learning in this context. The primary sources of data for the study were two semi-structured interviews that were conducted with each of the 36 students who volunteered to participate in the study (out of a total enrolment in the course of 45 students). The first interview focused on students' personal and family backgrounds, and general experience of coming to UCT to study chemical engineering. These interviews were conducted by Nazeema Ahmed, a qualified clinical psychologist, who was then working as a research assistant on the project. The second interview, which I conducted, focused more on the student's experience of the particular course: how they utilised the different learning activities in the course, how they felt about their performance on the different assessment events, and what they felt had helped or hindered their learning. The data therefore primarily reflect students' *accounts* of their learning experiences.

The first analysis conducted with these data aimed to provide a broad overview that encapsulated the student experience of learning in this context (Case 2007). An analytical framework centred on the sociological constructs of alienation and engagement was employed to that end, using a simple definition of alienation that evaluates whether an anticipated relationship is present or not. For example, most students expected to have some kind of relationship with their peers in the class, and the study showed that although many of them had small friendship groups with whom they engaged closely, they also desired to have connections with students across the class, and the absence of such relationships was characterised as a form of alienation. Likewise, many students expected to feel relevance and interest in what they were studying, but the huge workload meant that what they experienced was characterised more as drudgery and discipline – also termed a form of alienation here. Other alienated experiences were identified for some students with respect to their relationship to their families and their home, to the broader campus life and to their careers. A crucial finding in this study concerned the potentially powerful role of the lecturer in building relationships and alleviating alienation.

A further phase of the work employed James Gee's discourse analysis for a close interrogation of the interviews, working with Gee's notion of a 'Discourse model', an informal theory that people use to make sense of their world and their experiences (Gee 2005). This study identified what was termed the 'no problem Discourse model', where students present an upbeat portrayal of their experiences, diminishing the seriousness of the challenges they face academically (Case & Marshall 2008). Although this informal theory might be useful in buoying up their emotional state, it is seen to limit their ability to face up to the need to grapple closely with their work. This study also pointed to a further potentially crucial role for lecturers, who often when counselling students might be inclined to suggest that all will be fine in the end in an attempt to encourage students. This might unwittingly play into ongoing denial of the need for facing up to challenges.

Also emerging from this study is an article that presents an analysis of my own narrative, as a participant observer in this context (Case et al. 2010). Working together with two colleagues in the analysis, we were able to show the huge significance of the emotional dimension to the learning experience, especially in the context of having to build peer networks to accomplish academic work. In this analysis it is clearly noted that my experience in this regard could not be equivalent to that of a regular student, but it does deliver findings that offer further confirmation coming from a different angle on the earlier analyses.

A final journal article from this study started my work with narrative analysis, working with Sizwe's story, and thus prefiguring the directions for this book (Marshall & Case 2010). Narrative analysis here is seen as different to the more typical 'analysis of narrative', in which common themes are identified across data from a group. This definition, coming from the work of Donald Polkinghorne (1995), argues for the value of a form of analysis that considers the individual narrative closely on its own terms. This work builds on that of the psychologist Jerome Bruner (1985), who argued for 'narrative cognition' as a distinct knowledge mode, in contrast to that of (empiricist) science. In this article, narrative analysis of the first interview conducted with Sizwe was used to start to illustrate the value of this methodological direction. The issues raised in this analysis pointed to a significant rethink of how 'disadvantage' is commonly constructed in higher education, and these issues were signalled in the opening pages of this book.

In summary

Universities in South Africa were first established during the colonial period, intended at that time, as elsewhere, for the higher education of a largely white elite. During apartheid this system was entrenched for the older universities, with a segregated system offering separate and typically inferior university education for a small proportion of black South Africans. The new democracy has thus faced the enormous challenge both of attempting to equalise the quality of educational offerings across the system, as well as coping with a massive demand for increased participation, as common elsewhere across the globe. The twin issues of 'access' and 'success' signal the challenges at the level of student learning.

This case study is located within the chemical engineering programme at the University of Cape Town, one of the oldest universities, currently enjoying an impressive global ranking. Despite a longstanding focus on undergraduate education and a concomitant impressive output of a racially diverse body of graduates, concerns have remained about student success in this programme. The case study is located within this longstanding concern, and sought to understand the experience of student learning in the programme better. Over a semester during a third-year course, detailed data were gathered, significantly through two in-depth interviews with the majority of students enrolled in the course. Aspects of this study have been written up over the last period of time, and this present piece of work is a reanalysis of the data in social realist terms, in a format based on narrative methodology.

In a brief sketch we now have a geographical location for the case study – in social realist terms what we have started to sketch is the structural and cultural conditioning of the university space into which Sizwe and his classmates arrive when they start their studies in chemical engineering at the University of Cape Town.

However, this picture is incomplete without a view on the structural and cultural conditioning of engineering education. In the following chapter we will therefore take a closer look at the disciplinary area of engineering education, to consider the historical origins and contemporary issues in these programmes.

Notes

1 Small numbers of coloured students were offered 'permits' to study programmes at 'white' universities, which were not offered at 'coloured' universities.
2 'About UCT 2011–12', accessed at www.uct.ac.za.

Chapter 8

Disciplinary context for the study

Locating engineering education

What is distinct about the disciplinary space of engineering education that makes it different from other such spaces in the academy? This discussion starts with an outline of key debates in contemporary engineering education. These are then located within the historical trajectories that these programmes have followed in their establishment in the academy.

Current issues in engineering education

From a common-sense perspective, the starting point for any discussion on engineering education is fairly obvious: engineering education is surely simply about producing engineers. The only concerns then can be whether engineers are being produced in sufficient quantity and whether they have the requisite skills. And this two-sentence perspective, which can be noted in some of the earliest reports on engineering education (Prieto et al. 2009), can be easily identified across a wide range of current documents. There has been very little change in this general position over a long time now. The consensus is that there are insufficient students with the right academic backgrounds entering engineering programmes, and there is dissatisfaction with the relevance of the programmes towards the world of work. The discussion is always oriented towards changing the status quo.

It is most probably not surprising that the key players in the international discussion on engineering education are located in the wealthier countries, with the USA tending to be located (or at least locating itself) at the centre of this discussion. Other prominent voices, especially in the Anglophone world, are those of the UK and Australia. Three recent documents produced by professional bodies in these three countries, summarised in Table 8.1, provide a good place for starting to unpack some of the nuances in the debate.

The reader will be struck by the similarity in their titles: a definite sense of the millennial times and a strong orientation towards the future in the new century. Each report indeed grounds itself in a sense of the times in which we currently live. However, on closer inspection there are subtle variations across these three documents that reflect slightly different national contexts and concerns.

Table 8.1 Recent key documents produced by professional engineering bodies

Date	Title	Author(s)	Authoring body	Country
2004	*The engineer of 2020: Visions of engineering in the new century*	—	National Academy of Engineering (NAE)	USA
2006	*Educating engineers for the 21st century: The industry view*	Spinks, N., Silburn, N. & Birchall, D.	Royal Academy of Engineering (RAE)	UK
2008	*Engineers for the future*	King, R.	Australian Council of Engineering Deans (ACED)	Australia

The National Academy of Engineering (NAE) in the USA signals the fast pace of technological change as a central feature of the current context – theirs is a world of increased wealth and economic growth through a globalised economy (National Academy of Engineering 2004). A minor wrinkle on the horizon is noted with the occasional reference to the threat of terrorism and the impact of global outsourcing on local job prospects. In assessing future scenarios, those that are driven by technological change predominate. There is a recognition that natural disasters can interfere with this future, but an optimistic sense that technology can be developed to cope with risk. Overall the NAE's report gives an 'onwards and upwards' sense of things: 'Engineering has contributed enormously to the quality of life we enjoy today, and the opportunities for the future are likely to be ever greater' (p. 4).

A key focus for the NAE is on invigorating the public to share in its vision for engineering education. The desired attributes for the prospective graduates of 2020 do not seem to depart too drastically from those traditionally advocated: 'strong analytical skills, creativity, ingenuity, professionalism, and leadership' (National Academy of Engineering 2004: 5).

The report sponsored by the Royal Academy of Engineering (RAE) in the UK (Spinks et al. 2006) in its title signals directly that its focus is on an industry perspective. Thus this report involves relatively little assessment of the current context, and dives directly into a consideration of what skills industry needs both now and in the future. One key contextual feature is in the increase in offshoring of engineering jobs out of the UK and into countries that offer skilled personnel at lower wages. This is pushing UK engineering firms to concentrate more on high value-added products and activities. The increasing complexity of the management side of engineering work is also noted.

An interesting feature of the RAE report is the differentiation between 'high quality engineering graduates' and others who are presumably not of such high quality. Such a distinction is completely absent from the NAE report. The former group of high-quality graduates is considered to be globally comparable, and it is noted that firms also recruit internationally when needed. Throughout this report any reference to engineering 'graduates' is carefully qualified with reference to quality, 'appropriate skills', and so on. When questioned on what skills are needed in the future, again, as in the NAE report, there is not much change from the current perspective, which signals the need for specialised technical skills (including creativity and innovation) alongside interpersonal skills such as communication and team-work.

The report sponsored by the Australian Council of Engineering Deans (King 2008) is interesting to examine in the light of the other two reports. In this report there is a striking focus on the engineering education system itself, noting that in the somewhat more than a decade since a previous national report (Institution of Engineers of Australia 1996), many engineering schools had adopted substantial curriculum changes focused particularly towards the development of 'generic' graduate attributes, an increased use of 'problem-based learning' and its variants, and an increasing emphasis on sustainability and management. The current report notes that a hoped-for increase in the enrolment of engineering students, particularly with increased participation by women and other minority groups in engineering education, has not been achieved. The view is that the demand for engineers in Australia outstrips the supply. Moving towards the future, this perspective frames the discussion. The recommendations of this report are quite specific and include improving the quality of teaching and learning as well as improving the resources to deliver these programmes.

Looking across all three reports, it can be noted that despite some differences in framing of the 'national conversation', the common sense perspective outlined at the opening of this chapter predominates: engineering education is there to produce engineers for industry. Are we producing sufficient engineers? Do they have the requisite skills? The inclusion of a focus towards women and minorities in the Australian report is primarily located in a concern around the supply of engineering graduates. These are, of course, reports put out by professional bodies and thus – clearly – are representing the interests of the profession. The same position, though, frames the contemporary discussion among most engineering academics, as can be seen in any perusal of journal papers or conference proceedings.

Engineering education is located in a knowledge area termed a *region* by Bernstein (2000), looking both outwards towards the profession and inwards towards the academy. To start to understand this particular location we thus need to go back and trace the origins of both the profession and the formal educational arrangements that arose alongside it.

The origins of engineering education in the academy

Although a popular view might wish to trace the engineering profession all the way back to the Pyramids, if one is taking a definition of a profession as a distinct body of individuals who take charge of a particular domain of knowledge for the purposes of practice in society, then one can say that engineers came into being with the industrial revolution. The development of manufacturing industry and the erection of large-scale public works projects during this period were accomplished by individuals who had a wide variety of formal educational back-grounds, if any, although there were a range of systems of apprenticeships 'on the job'. The early 'engineers' were businessmen, entrepreneurs, skilled craftsmen, sci-entists; they started to become distinguished by what they could do (and started to identify themselves in that way) rather than through any formal credentials. During the mid- to late nineteenth century modern engineering really took off, with the emergence of science-based industry, termed by the sociologist David Noble 'the wedding of science to the useful arts' (Noble 1977). The newer disciplines of elec-trical and chemical engineering arose in this period, building on the development of an electricity network and the petrochemicals industry, and the older disciplines of civil and mechanical engineering were substantially modified.

Starting in the late nineteenth century in the USA and somewhat later in Britain and her colonies the provision of formal engineering education started to move from a small set of idiosyncratic qualifications mostly outside the academy into a widespread provision of programmes largely in the universities. Engineering had a particular struggle to obtain recognition within the then largely classically ori-ented colleges. A strategic move to obtain respectability was to align themselves with science, and indeed Noble (1977) notes that in the USA the development of engineering programmes had an effect on the science that was being practised in the colleges, moving it towards the more empirical. But the effect of all these competing forces on the nascent engineering programmes was substantial: the location in the academy saw the rise of engineering science as well as the inclu-sion of humanities-type courses in the engineering programme. Reflecting on this scenario, Noble notes that:

> The efforts of the engineering educators to meet the demands of their pro-fession, academic status, and employers of engineers were never wholly sat-isfactory. Indeed, the problems have remained the focus of their concern throughout the twentieth century.
>
> (Noble 1977: 28)

On the European continent, in Germany in particular, formal provision of engineering education has a slightly longer history, with the establishment of engineering (technical) colleges (*technische hochschulen*) that were indepen-dent of the existing university system, alongside a separate and more practically oriented system (*fachhochschulen*). The same tensions, however, between science and practice, can be noted in individual institutions over the nineteenth century, with an ultimate trend towards what can be termed 'academization' (Harwood 2006), where science and the interests of the academy got the upper hand over the concerns of industry. The situation in France was slightly different, where from the outset a strongly differentiated national system was established, with some institutions designated to offer a more mathematical and scientific engineering education while others were mandated to be more practical. Ultimately, though, the trend towards academisation can be noted even at the latter institutions.

Comparing across continents, it is important to note that European-trained engineers coming into the USA in the interwar period found the American training to be comparatively less theoretical; in due course some commentators have identified the influx of European engineers into the US academy as a key factor in intensifying the theoretical focus of the degree from the middle of the twentieth century onwards (Harwood 2006). Another key factor, of course, was the massive increase in federal funding for scientific research in the post-war period.

From the earliest days there was a pushback from the industrial world, where concerns were voiced that the graduates of these programmes did not have the skills needed to function in the engineering workplace. Through a range of professional organisations, working engineers sought to exert pressure on engineering programmes to adapt to their needs. In the range of programmes that had been established in the USA and the UK in the nineteenth century some institutions had sought to include the 'shop culture' of the apprentices through, for example, a 'sandwich' scheme, while others (typically the more elite institutions) had developed programmes that were more closely aligned to science (Harwood 2006). By the early twentieth century it was the latter type of programmes that predominated, although engineering academics had started to develop a distinctive 'engineering science'. The first substantial report on engineering education in the USA, the Mann Report, focused itself towards 'the new corporate industrial reorientation of engineering education' (Mann 1918). Noble notes:

> The professionalization of engineering and the establishment of engineering education as a recognized branch of higher learning forged a link between the corporation and the university that remains unbroken to this day.
>
> (Noble 1977: xii)

The history of the engineering profession itself is thus also pertinent to a consideration of engineering education. Some early commentators, most notably Thorsten Veblen, had assumed that engineers as professionals would retain their independence and that indeed there would be in due course a conflict between the engineers' devotion to technical concerns and the managers' focus on profits. This, famously, never came about, since engineers started to orient their professional status towards success in the corporation and occupation of senior level managerial roles. This is a very different conception of professional identity compared to the older professions like medicine and law who locate their identity in the possession of a specialised body of knowledge. The engineering profession developed in such a way that it ended up aligning itself almost entirely with the interests of corporate capital and took its identity and cues from this set of interests. This is especially so for the newer engineering disciplines, for example chemical engineering, which, argues Colin Divall, needed to differentiate themselves from chemistry and mechanical engineering, and thus developed 'a much closer and less troubled relationship with business ideals than in the older engineering specialties' (Divall 1994: 259).

Noble sees this development as inevitable given the reliance of engineers on large corporations in order to be able to practise their profession, but also, significantly, owing to the extraordinary success of twentieth-century US-centred global capitalism. Tracing the development of engineering professional identity, Noble notes that over time engineers came to be 'fully domesticated'. The extent of their critique and independence from the corporation ended over discussions of the individual pay packet. It is important too to recognise, as Noble emphasises, that the leading engineers of the early twentieth century saw themselves, through their corporations, as advancing a new and more civilised society. The rhetoric of engineering as central to offering a better quality of life to all citizenry was central to their thinking as 'corporate liberals' (Noble 1977).

Calls for reform of engineering education

In a 1995 report on engineering education, the chairman of the National Academy of Engineering, Norman Augustine, reviewed all the major US reports on engineering education that came out in the twentieth century, starting with the Wickenden Report of 1930, and concluded: 'It is startling to read them and recognize the consistency of many of their themes across the decades' (Board on Engineering Education 1995: 5). He lists these as:

- the need for strong grounding in the fundamentals of mathematics and the physical and engineering sciences;
- the importance of design and laboratory experimentation;
- a call for more attention to the development of communication and social skills in engineers;
- the need for integration of social and economic studies and liberal arts into the curriculum;
- the vital importance of good teaching and attention to curriculum development; and
- the need to prepare students for career-long learning.

Augustine does, however, note that the relative importance of these various themes can be seen to shift over the changing social and economic contexts of the USA through the twentieth century. The post-war period (reflected in the Grinter Report of 1955) resulted in a massively increased emphasis on mathematics and science in the engineering curriculum, following the wartime significance of scientifically advanced engineering solutions. Since the 1960s, however, there has been little change in the basic structure of engineering degrees in the USA, UK and related contexts (although of course there is always local variation and there have been programmes of modest innovation in some places). In recent times there has thus been an intensification of calls for reform of the engineering curriculum.

What does this curriculum look like? The earlier years are generally devoted to basic sciences, including mathematics, with the engineering sciences being introduced alongside these in the second year of study. Senior years involve advanced study in engineering sciences as well as more project-based courses including design. Some programmes have introduced introductory engineering courses into the first year. Some curriculum reforms have seen an introduction of project-based courses throughout the curriculum, with a more radical version being the delivery of all courses in a problem-based learning format where students go and find the knowledge they need to solve a particular problem and engage in facilitated small group exercises to achieve this. This is, however, quite unusual, and thus most engineering programmes are largely comprised of courses that involve the teaching of a particular area of science or engineering science and where students get assessed on their ability to complete close-ended problems that require an application of the science, usually in an examination situation. Engineering programmes tend to carry a relatively large course load of this type, alongside practical or project courses.

The perspectives from the professional bodies have been introduced above. In advanced economies there remains a concern about the levels of enrolment in engineering programmes, especially (in the USA) among its own citizens. Since at least the 1960s there have been ongoing investigations and reports on the relatively low level of participation in engineering studies by women. This work forms part of a larger literature on gender and Science, Technology, Engineering and Mathematics (STEM) careers more generally. As noted above, most of the concern from the engineering profession has been about this issue as part of a larger concern for numbers, while most reports in the scholarly literature are motivated by concerns for gender equity as a fundamentally desirable end in itself. Responses span the range from 'girl-friendly' initiatives through to more feminist perspectives that question the very structure and nature of engineering in gender terms (Stonyer 2002). The calls for increased participation by women in engineering have been somewhat matched by a concern around the enrolment of students of colour, with much of this work originating in the USA during the civil rights era, followed later by a substantial contribution towards the end of apartheid in South Africa. Despite a plethora of reports and a multitude of initiatives, it has to be noted at this point, some fifty years on, that, in the advanced economies of the West, most of the traditional engineering disciplines remain a predominantly white male space, with growing participation by Asian students. There are some engineering disciplines, for example chemical engineering, and a range of newer engineering disciplines that are biologically focused, that have high enrolments of women, but this tends to show in stark relief how little has changed in the traditional domains of mechanical, electrical and civil engineering. With regard to the participation of black students in engineering in the USA, a recent report shows that participation has recently stalled, with a minor peak in 2000 of 5.7 per cent (compared to a demographic representation of 13 per cent of the US population) to about 5.3 per cent currently (Slaton 2010). By comparison, in the USA, women's overall share of bachelor's degrees in engineering has risen dramatically from 25 per cent in the 1960s to

50 per cent currently (with much of this growth, as noted above, coming from the 'newer' engineering disciplines).

The professional world continues to question the relevance of the qualification, as it has done since the earliest days of engineering education. Many of these contemporary concerns, however, are located within an understanding that the world of engineering work has changed and continues to do so, and that the 1960s curriculum, which focuses predominantly on the acquisition of engineering science knowledge, is potentially out of touch with the current context. Jorgensen (2007) makes the important point that although the theory–practice debate is an old one, the nature of the theoretical knowledge and the practical skills under discussion has changed radically over this period of more than a century.

Some of this concern is located within a sense that engineers are becoming nothing more than skilled technical workers. This, of course, should not be surprising given the historical development of the profession outlined above in which engineers made their professional status subordinate to the interests of the corporation. In these arguments there is a concern that engineers should have the education that will enable them to take on leadership roles in society rather than being servants to business people. Jorgensen writes:

> Although engineers' identity as creators and designers is supported in histori-
> cal writing and in strategic reports about the role of engineering in the future,
> reality seems to place engineers in roles closer to analysts and scientists in
> laboratories and modern technical industries.
>
> (Jørgensen 2007: 234)

An argument coming from a different angle suggests that it is the contemporary needs of society that require a differently educated engineer, one who has engaged with a much broader knowledge base. Domenico Grasso and colleagues term this 'holistic engineering', which they define as follows:

> It is an approach that recognizes that engineering's greatest and most immedi-
> ate challenge for the 21st century is no longer solely how to train capable tech-
> nical experts – the engineering leadership niche in the manufacturing economy
> – but how to cultivate professionals able to take on the most complex tech-
> nological, social challenges that did not exist even 20 years ago, ranging from
> mitigating climate change through smart grid technologies to securing health
> records and financial markets in an increasingly inter-connected world.
>
> (Grasso & Burkins 2009: 2)

In this perspective we also have a view that contemporary engineering problems inherently involve social and political issues and need to speak to challenges that are global and not just national. Grasso and Martinelli speak powerfully to the position prevalent in much US engineering education discussion that focuses primarily on national competitiveness:

The emergence of a new global engineering work force and its threat to the US economy has been the topic du jour in engineering and business circles, but responses tend to focus on increasing the number of traditional engineering graduates so we can go head-to-head with other countries in the technological marketplace. Such a goal alone, however, would do little more than drive down the price and value of engineering services, leaving the United States no better equipped than other nations to solve the increasingly complex problems facing society.

(Grasso & Martinelli 2009: 12)

They argue that an engineering degree with greater perceived as well as actual relevance is also needed to attract the current generation of potential engineering students, especially those from a diverse range of cultural backgrounds. They note that over a period where other professions such as medicine and law have substantially diversified their student base, engineering has languished, for example, with a comparatively low participation of women in many parts of the world. They argue that this is related at least in part to a lack of a perception of the social relevance of engineering, compared to other professions.

Resonating with the work of Nussbaum outlined in the previous chapter, Grasso and Martinelli then proceed to argue that:

To better serve humanity, engineers must at least attempt to understand the human condition in all its complexity, which requires the study of literature, history, philosophy, psychology, religion, and economics, among other fields.

(Grasso & Martinelli 2009: 13)

In his vision of a renewed professional education, William Sullivan also points to the nature of complex twenty-first-century challenges, writing that:

For professionals to deal with problems such as these, they have to amend the distanced stance of the technical expert with the more engaged role of the civic professional. This means entering as a participant and learning from, as well as about, the networks of meaning and connection in which people live. It often means exerting leadership to gather and deploy resources and people to improve situations.

(Sullivan 2011: 114)

These calls for reform towards a professional degree that is more in step with contemporary challenges can be described in Archer's terms as questions about the possibilities for *morphogenesis*: for changing the shape of things. It has been noted that engineering education has been largely unchanged over at least the last fifty years, and the broader conversation in which it takes place shows continuity from its origins in the nineteenth century – this scenario is characterised by Archer's notion of *morphostasis*. The case study to be shortly presented is located within these debates. It certainly needs to build a strong explanatory view on the current state of student learning in a typical engineering programme, but it also needs to use this explanation to be able to understand the space in which we work in order to carefully assess the possibilities and the potential trade-offs for change.

In summary

This chapter commenced with an examination of the current debates in the world of engineering education: around enrolments in engineering programmes, around graduation rates in these programmes, and on the career choices made by successful graduates. These concerns were thereafter given a historical context by a tracing of the origins of engineering education in the academy. Here we are able to locate the longstanding tensions between industry and the academy on what students should learn in an engineering degree and how this relates to the world of engineering practice. In short, despite a few tussles in the late nineteenth and early twentieth century, it can be seen that across the globe, in high-status institutions, the interests of the academy have predominated. Engineering curricula are strongly oriented towards engineering science, and have limited engagement with the world of practice.

The final section in this chapter considered the calls for reform of the engineering curriculum that have been periodically issued over time. Two somewhat related strands were identified: first, building on the historical tension between theory and practice mentioned above, many reformers have called for a curriculum that has greater relevance to the world of work. Second, coming from a different angle around social inclusion and race and gender equity, other reformers have called a curriculum that might be experienced as more inclusive. In many cases these two arguments become somewhat interlinked, with an argument that a more 'relevant' curriculum would be more appealing to a greater diversity of students.

In the ongoing laments about the degree to which engineering graduates are or are not prepared for the world of work, there is an assumption that there should be a tight fit between the knowledge in the university degree and the knowledge needed in the workplace. In this space of recontextualisation there is a contestation between different power interests, as seen so clearly in the history of engineering education, with the competing interests of the academic world and the world of the engineering profession. In Archerian terms, we can note situational logics of contradiction at the time of establishment of the early engineering programmes as discussed above, with a fairly wide range of programmes on offer in which some were closely aligned to the shop floor and others had more points of similarity with the science degrees that already existed in the academy. We have now arrived at a situation where there is such a wide degree of similarity in engineering degrees across much of the globe that a system of mutual accreditation has come into play. It is argued here that what has happened is a form of accommodation in which a degree system that satisfies the needs for legitimation in the academic sphere has evolved, but is also accepted and accredited by the professional world (albeit with periodic contestation over its relevance).

Thus we can see that the structural and cultural conditioning of the peda-gogical space in engineering education takes place at many levels. With a his-torical backdrop of the evolution of engineering education within the academy, it has been shown that a progressive accommodation of contradictory interests has led to the engineering curriculum that we encounter today. This curriculum then takes on life in actual courses, which are 'delivered' in particular contexts by individual lecturers. The space that these lecturers inhabit as employees of the academy is itself conditioned so that the space in which they teach has notable constraints and some enablements. We are now in a position to 'start the clock' and to focus on the trajectory of individual students as they move through engi-neering studies, and it is to a consideration of these events that we turn in the following chapters.

Chapter 9

Choosing engineering

At this point we are ready to insert the students as human agents into this space and to start the morphogenetic clock ticking. Working within a temporal sequence, this chapter starts charting students' engagement with engineering education during the process in which students make choices to study engineering. As noted earlier, this is one of the key concerns in debates on engineering education as engineering appears to continue to decline in popularity, particularly in the Western world.

Debates on student enrolment in engineering programmes

It has been noted earlier that the demand for access to higher education, globally, continues to grow exponentially. This is especially so in emerging economies with rapidly growing middle classes who are seeking access to higher education, notably in India and China. In engineering education the issues of enrolment play out in particular ways. In much of the West there is an ongoing concern about the absolute numbers of students enrolling in engineering, noting that this often appears a relatively unattractive choice of study. A recent meta-analysis identified 30 published reports on this matter in just the first decade of this century (Prieto et al. 2009). In these countries the push towards widening participation in engineering education is often framed in terms of gender, although in the USA there has also been a longstanding concern about the participation of under-represented ethnic groups.

These discussions lead inevitably to an exhortation for better marketing of the engineering profession, to get the word out to top scholars that this is an attractive career. Yet despite whatever efforts are made in these directions, little is seen to change. Amid this usual rhetoric, one recent article stands out in tackling the issue head-on. Frank Stefan Becker from the Association for German Engineers asks an apparently simple question in a paper entitled: 'Why don't young people want to become engineers? Rational reasons for disappointing decisions' (Becker 2010). Rather than assuming, as is usually done that these young people are either misguided, ignorant or have insufficient information on hand, he takes a fresh look and provides a rational response to this phenomenon 'even at the risk of debunking some common myths and presenting unpleasant truths' (p. 350). In his analysis, he suggests that students are making a rational comparison with other careers on offer in these largely post-industrialised economies, and that the engineering career is simply not very attractive. Moreover, the clear link between technology and the improvement of human life that was so much in evidence from the nineteenth century until well into the twentieth no longer holds in advanced industrialised economies. On this point, Becker perceptively notes that the situation is indeed different in emerging economies, and he refers to recent survey studies, such as that by Sjøberg and colleagues, which show a completely different pattern in terms of young people's interest in getting a job 'in technology' (Sjøberg et al. 2010).

Drawing on literature that shows the cyclical nature of the demand for engineers as matching the economic situation, Becker notes soberly that the large numbers of unemployed engineers in Germany during the 1990s is a reality of which young people making career decisions are not unaware. He argues that the national rhetoric around skills shortages needs always to be interrogated closely. From a German perspective, he argues that highly specialised undergraduate degrees are risky in a climate where broad-based engineers are likely to have better employment prospects. Finally, he notes that, contrary to what might be expected if there really were a demand for engineers and a sustained shortage, engineering salaries across the globe have generally shown a relative decline over the last few decades. Furthermore, for those students who have what he describes as a 'post-materialist' attitude and who are not motivated by salary, other careers, including more environmentally oriented science degrees, tend to be preferred.

Researching the choice to study engineering

So what do we know about the students who are choosing engineering, in both rich and poor countries? We will start with some evidence from South African engineering students, who to some degree represent a straddling of these two worlds. Some fifteen years ago, my colleague Jeff Jawitz and I asked just over 500 first years to produce a short open-ended piece in which they described why they had chosen to study engineering (Jawitz & Case 1998). In line with much research at the time, our thinking was very much around 'factors' that influenced students' choices. We were particularly interested in the reasons outlined by black students and by female students, given our focus towards increasing the participation of these groups in engineering. Much of our study replicated the typical findings that other international studies had generated and which reflected a lot of the common-sense thinking about engineering: students choose these careers for the salary prospects, some are motivated by science, others are motivated by doing something practical and the involvement of significant others like parents and teachers in this decision is substantial. Something that struck us in the study, however, was the emergence of a new theme that we had not seen elsewhere. We noted that some students, particularly black students, provided motivations for studying engineering that related to the social and political context. They were motivated to make a change in their community, and they were also motivated to be making a mark in a career that was traditionally white and male. These data were collected in 1996, only a few years after the transition to a democratic government in South Africa, and before the tumultuous 2000s on the world stage. It is thus particularly interesting to put these findings in conversation with a study recently conducted with UK engineering students.

Esat Alpay and colleagues at Imperial College, one of the top-ranked international engineering institutions, surveyed their incoming engineering students on their 'aspirations'. It should be noted here, of course, that a question on 'aspirations' is slightly different from 'reasons for choosing engineering', but the results resonate in interesting ways. In checking off from a list of potential 'aspirations', three responses predominated: inventing something new, making a difference to the world and achieving financial security. Alpay and colleagues noted that the aspiration towards invention was particularly pronounced for male students and that making a difference was significant among female students. They also surveyed engineering students across the years on these same aspirations, and it is interesting to note that the pattern is roughly unchanged until the final year, when concerns of financial security shoot up and the aspiration to invent something declines to a very low response rate. The proportion of the class who aspire to make a difference is unchanged at about a quarter.

Moving to a social realist perspective

These broad brushstroke surveys are tantalising in hinting at pertinent issues, but do not take us very far in any in-depth understanding of how actual students mobilise such reasons and make choices. Part of the problem is that in this discussion so far we are using simplistic models of causality that analyse reasons or aspirations as 'factors' influencing career choice and look for overall prevalence and correlations. As noted earlier, Archer's social realist theory offers a view on individual agency that is underpinned by a critical realist perspective that encompasses a more complex model of causality in the social world, built upon a particular ontology, outlined earlier in Chapter 3 (see pp. 37–39). The observable objective world is the world of the *actual*, but if we assume that that is all there is we end up with very limited explanations of social phenomena.

An important move that has been taken up across much interpretivist-inspired education research has been the move to the level of the *empirical*, which is the world of subjective experience. We obtain a very important perspective on education when we start to consider our courses not only from the viewpoint of what we as lecturers intend, but crucially from the perspective of how students perceive the experience and how they make sense of it. From a critical realist perspective, however, this move is still insufficient. If we remain at the level of understanding students' experiences we certainly might, as individual lecturers, develop some more empathy. However, if, as scholars, we wish to know how to really effect positive change, we will be limited to exhorting our colleagues to greater empathy, with limited effect. To understand more completely the constraints and enablements with which the social world presents us, we need to complete the realist analysis and make the move to the level of the *real* in which the mechanisms of structure and culture are located.

Using this perspective, we would note that the decision to choose engineering is located in a broader structural and cultural context, some of which has been sketched out so far. However, we need now to focus on individual student agency, since what is clear is that individuals with the same social contexts do not necessarily make the same choices. At the same time, we need to also recognise that the choice to engage with higher education has a substantially higher cost (not just financial) attached to it, particularly so for some individuals compared to others. Archer's theory allows us to account for the different patterns in which people make choices. Crucially, we need to see the decision to participate in a particular course of study as a 'substantive personal project'; moreover this project can be seen as 'part of a wider process to establish or re-establish oneself in a specific way of life' (Kahn 2009: 264).

How do people make these decisions? Archer argues for the central role of what she terms the *internal conversation*, and it is reflexivity that describes the different ways in which people carry out their conversations. As noted earlier (pp. 59–60), *communicative reflexivity* involves externalising your decisions through discussions with others. By contrast, *autonomous reflexives* hold their internal conversations without much need for outside input, and they formulate personal projects that are focused towards achieving high levels of competence in their chosen skills. *Meta-reflexives* are quite different and tend to focus their internal conversations around social ideals. They formulate projects in relation to their dissatisfaction with the social circumstances of others.

Exploring student narratives of choice

The preface to this book introduced Sizwe's story. In his initial explanation of how Sizwe came to be studying engineering it is clear that this was indeed a substantial project, which was aimed at changing the circumstances in which he and his orphaned siblings lived. He started to recognise that he had strong academic ability and decided to use this as the basis for his project. He had seen an article that had featured a successful black engineer, and this gave him the feeling that he could do it too. Engineering also became the means by which he obtained bursary funding for university studies. This is the classic story of an autonomous reflexive. At the conclusion of his interview, though, Sizwe gives us a sense of his growing meta reflexivity in that he does not see himself fitting into a standard corporate job and wants to find a way of doing something for the community.

Let us now consider the stories of a few of Sizwe's classmates. Their biographical details are summarised in Table 9.1. Phumzile's father had passed away when

Table 9.1 Biographical details of students in Chapter 9

	Grew up in	*Brought up by*	*Schooled at*	*Funding for studies*
Sizwe	township	orphaned in high school, becomes child head of family	township state school	bursary
Phumzile	township	mother (father deceased)	low-fee private church school	bursary
Susan	suburb	mother and father	traditional private school	parents
Cyril	lower middle-class suburb	mother and father	multiracial state school	parents

she was very young and she was brought up by her mother together with an older brother. She lived in an urban township and attended a (private but relatively low-fee) church school that was considered a cut above the local township schools (see brief outline on p. 68 for the schooling landscape in post-apartheid South Africa). In discussing her study choice Phumzile said that when she was growing up she wanted to be a doctor or a lawyer, but was put off on the one hand by 'blood and stuff' and on the other hand by the experience of writing history essays. She said she considered a range of careers and then thought 'Okay, let me try engineering.' In deciding which engineering discipline to select her teacher said 'Most girls go for Chem', and so she applied for chemical engineering at UCT – her choice of university was because most of her friends were going to the University of the Witwatersrand (in Johannesburg) and she felt she needed to go and meet new people.

In earlier research with female students who had the qualifications but had not chosen to do engineering, we had identified this very pattern where for some students engineering is what is left over when the other professional careers, most notably medicine, have been eliminated (Jawitz et al. 2000). Phumzile's desire is to get a professional qualification, and she selects engineering on this basis, without too much further thought on what it might entail. Strikingly, she makes a decision to remove herself from her immediate community and to head to a university at the other end of the country. In this narrative we can identify aspects of autonomous reflexivity.

Susan comes from a middle-class suburban white family with a father who worked as an engineer. She attended a private girls' school and had a sense at that stage that her talents were in the academic sphere. She had two original 'big passions': one was to be a chemistry lecturer and the other a history teacher. She decided that a history teacher was not a great career choice and so started exploring chemistry a bit. At a local university open day she got talking to someone from chemical engineering who showed her that this discipline still involved the maths and science ('quite heavy') but with a lot broader career opportunities. She decided that she would then go for this direction, which she felt would 'open more doors'. This short narrative graphically illustrates the much larger base of information and opportunities that a middle-class context offers for the making of a career choice. Interestingly, Susan starts off with a relatively intrinsic desire to do teaching and is then persuaded to take a direction that will offer more extrinsic options. Further on in the interview Susan says that she still reads widely and enjoys the humanities but is happy with her choice: 'What we're learning has a purpose; we're going to use it and apply it.' Knowing that by the end of her third year Susan has decided that she cannot see herself working as an engineer lends towards the interpretation that in some ways this study choice did not emerge from a completely autonomous decision but was rather influenced by a view 'out there' that one should do something useful, an act of communicative reflexivity.

Cyril comes from a black (termed 'coloured' during apartheid, referring to persons of mixed-race descent) lower-middle-class family living locally in Cape Town with his parents and siblings. His mother worked as a university administrator at another university and he had decided he wanted to get a university degree and that he would aim for UCT, which seemed desirable. He enjoyed mathematics and science at school and had decided to do engineering ('I enjoyed the logical way engineering works'), but then he said he became 'kind of scared', especially when talking to guidance counsellors who suggested he do actuarial science because he was good at mathematics. He did the first year of actuarial science, decided it 'wasn't for him' and changed over to chemical engineering. Here we can see clearly the difficulty of wrenching oneself from a communicative to an autonomous mode of reflexivity.

What we can see across these narratives is that the social context in which a student finds himself or herself conditions the options that they can consider. For all of these students they found themselves performing well at school, and that put them into the category where they could legitimately consider access to university and to degrees with high entrance criteria. However, the broader family and community context further conditioned the options at hand, in terms of possibilities and opportunity costs. Students without family funding needed to consider getting a bursary, and engineering is one of the few areas with strong bursary options. From a township background the actual choice of degree was not something around which there were many possibilities to engage; the simple thing was of getting a degree that would afford a different lifestyle. Getting to university involved a massive step of autonomy and moving out of the community in which they had grown up. Susan and Cyril were both from family backgrounds that, even though having different material resources, had an easier connection to the possibilities of university study. These two found themselves in the different situation of being able to explore a range of options and how these might or might not match their interests; interestingly, both of them ended up being persuaded not to go for their initial choice, and notably for both of them there was a range of choices.

In summary

We can now see the paucity of a 'model' of career choices that lines up a set of factors and sees which are predominant. Although, as noted earlier, this has thrown up issues that might not have been easily perceived, in these analyses we lose sight of the individual and the complex emergent processes whereby a course of actions becomes embarked upon. This is not a set of particles moving through a pipeline that make the grade through a filter into the next stage of the pipeline.

Importantly, reflexivity, although a characteristic of the individual agent, is located strongly within the options that are at hand with their associated costs, which depend strongly on the cultural and material resources in the context. Thus for those with limited finance the option of a bursary to study engineering is a key consideration, while those from more middle-class backgrounds are able to survey a wide range of options and attempt to match something to their emerging interests – although this process is not without its difficulties too. In exercising reflexivity we see here that for those from relatively deprived backgrounds, the choice to study engineering at a top university is by definition a choice that rests on autonomous reflexivity, the creation of desires and aspirations that are not defined by the context of one's birth. On the other hand, there is some evidence of communicative reflexivity among those from more privileged backgrounds – the difficulty of finding one's one path amid the inevitability of heading to university.

Thus, we should not move to thinking – as is so often the case with a variety of psychological-type constructs – that we could simply work out a way to select the individuals with the 'right' reflexivity for engineering education and proceed from there. We can see how the same choice – to study engineering – can be made at the end of a range of different deliberative paths located in particular contexts. This is the start of a journey of crafting a *modus vivendi* – a way of living. Reflexivity is not a set characteristic and thus we should expect that in the transition to higher education – for many students a shift away from their immediate natal context – we will note changes in reflexivity and ongoing crafting and recrafting of possibilities. We pick up this story again in the following chapter.

Chapter 10

Studying engineering
Defining your project

Many students who enter engineering do not qualify in these programmes. What is it about engineering that makes this such a tough degree? Here we start to map out the experience of studying engineering, noting what it means to make this your 'project'.

Academic success in engineering studies

The pipeline metaphor has some of its particles leaking out along the way and others making it to the end. Some students succeed and others do not. The engineering education pipeline is a very leaky one. Proceeding along this direction many sophisticated quantitative analyses have been done of student success. We can get an overall sense of what proportion of students do succeed in their chosen programmes – and in most contexts we will find this a disturbing statistic. The Australian Council of Engineering Deans' report mentioned earlier notes that of Australian males entering engineering programmes, only 52 per cent graduate, while the corresponding figure for female students is 60 per cent (King 2008). In South Africa a study mentioned earlier (Scott et al. 2007) shows that, five years after entry, only 54 per cent of students had completed the four-year bachelor's programme in engineering, while 19 per cent were still studying and the remainder had dropped out or been academically excluded.

We can try to correlate 'success' with other 'variables', and we will note, as has been noted in so many different education systems, that one of the best (but not perfect) predictors of future academic success is past academic success. We can also note that students from more privileged backgrounds, on average, succeed at a greater rate than those who do not come from these backgrounds. There is a lot of important research that has been done to quantify these kinds of issues, but it does not typically lead one towards a view on how to change the typical system outcomes.

Researching the student experience of learning

How can we get at the student experience of studying engineering? The research design that one chooses obviously determines the kind of data that can be obtained. A recent large-scale survey study in the USA set out to explore the engineering student experience (Sheppard 2009). Students at 21 engineering institutions were invited to participate in the 'APPLES' survey; a 14 per cent response rate generated quantitative data from a relatively representative sample of over 4,000 students on their motivations for studying engineering, how they experienced their education and what their post-graduation plans were.

By definition, this kind of research design generates a particular sort of finding – the value is in the broad brushstroke and in the ability to show relationships between particular reported experiences, as well as with aspects such as junior or senior status in the programme. Thus, it is reported that students are 'generally satisfied' with the quality of their educational experience. It is interesting and maybe not surprising to note that the frequency of the student's reported interaction with their lecturer is positively correlated with the overall self-reported degree of satisfaction. This study finds that a sense of 'curriculum overload' is negatively correlated with the student's Grade Point Average (GPA), echoing earlier work by Ramsden (2003). Thus, as might well be expected, students who are performing well academically are generally feeling more on top of their work and able to cope. A further correlation is that those students who are experiencing overload (and producing weaker GPAs) are also those who report concerns over financing their education. This study continues to produce findings of this sort: although senior students report greater interaction with their instructors (as one might expect given the way the engineering curriculum progresses towards final year with more project work), they are also less satisfied with their instructors and overall less engaged with their studies. The latter finding is more pronounced for women, and especially pronounced for women from under-represented minorities.

Moving towards a social realist approach

As important as good quantitative data can be for offering a particular perspective on engineering education, going along this avenue of inquiry does not take one far enough for getting any real sense of what is happening in the system. Studies such as the APPLES survey mentioned here are useful in offering some kind of overall sense of the engineering landscape but are limited in building explanatory theory. Furthermore, in working with a close-ended survey there is frustratingly little sense of the real student. Archer describes this mode of social research as a 'blunt instrument' (Archer 2003: 143). In this chapter, with her sharper analytical tools in hand, a different perspective will be developed on what is happening 'inside' the system of engineering education.

It is fair enough to start off with a focus on the individual student, since the success of the individual is an important event which, aggregated, gives the outcome for the whole system. However, if, as in much student learning research to date, we limit our focus to the student and their abilities/actions/motivations/behaviours we obtain a distorted picture of what is happening. If we see student learning as a simple causal outcome of teaching we will also fail to grasp the full picture. Working within the morphogenetic framework, we need to see student learning as the outcome of a complex set of interactions, in the relations between students, teachers and other students, in the interactions between individual students and the cultural system of engineering knowledge, and in the ways in which these relations are conditioned by the broader world of structural and cultural influences.

To account fully for the development of student agency, as noted in Chapter 6, we need to explore both *personal identity* and *social identity*. In the first instance here, considering the individual student and their choices as they proceed through engineering studies, we will attempt to characterise personal identity. Personal identity (see pp. 57–59) is centred on the *internal conversation* and in what we decide to care about, our 'constellation of concerns' (Archer 2007c: 40). What we care about and how we decide to proceed with regard to that is the formulation of a project. Humans typically are engaged in more than one project simultaneously – in fact to entirely neglect concerns in one order is to risk your well-being in the others. In resolving this dilemma we achieve a *modus vivendi*, a way in which we will go about our being in the world. Here we need to manage a multitude of concerns, but we also need to disaggregate some sense of our *ultimate concerns*, the things that matters to us most and which are long-term objectives.

Exploring student narratives of studying engineering

To get a sense of what is happening in this space, we look at the narratives from Sizwe and his classmates about what they are experiencing as they are doing the third-year course in advanced reactor engineering. At the outset of the book we noted that Sizwe's emerging personal identity sees him set himself apart from the typical chemical engineering student in that he refused for his life to be completely dominated by his chemical engineering studies and he managed to incorporate other forms of involvement. Sizwe describes this mentality that he saw in others and continually pushed against thus: 'when you do anything else apart from studying, actually you are wasting time.'

We now turn to consider the other students whose narratives were introduced in the previous chapter, and thereafter further students will be brought into the pool. The biographical details of the full group to be considered in this chapter are summarised in Table 10.1.

Susan, who was introduced in the previous chapter when she was choosing chemical engineering over chemistry, is at this point in third year the top student in the class, and she says: 'The thing is, learning chem eng is not fun, it really isn't like, it's tons and tons of maths, and all you have to do is work, and it takes over your whole life.'

Table 10.1 Biographical details of students in Chapter 10

	Grew up in	Brought up by	Schooled at	Funding for studies
Sizwe	township	orphaned in high school, becomes child head of family	township state school	bursary
Phumzile	township	mother (father deceased)	low-fee private church school	bursary
Susan	suburb	mother and father	traditional private school	parents
Cyril	lower middle-class suburb	mother and father	multiracial state school	parents
Rajesh	foreign African country	mother and father	selective public school, completed A-levels	parents
Sibongile	rural area	parents divorced in high school, lives with father	rural state boarding school	bursary
Peter	suburb	mother and father	multiracial state school	parents

She described in a humorous manner always having to turn down a simple invitation to have tea with the girl in the flat opposite her because, as she said 'well, I can't bring my computer with me'! Susan said:

> But, I have all those things as well which are, they're a part of my life and they're not, this is the thing: chem eng takes over your life, it's terrible, that's the worst thing about it. Is just not having time to do, to expand your life in any way. To think outside the chem eng box.

Here she is expressing the conflict she has in trying to resolve what matters to her – her concerns – with the structural implications of her choice of chemical engineering. Phumzile, who was encountered previously when she selected engineering over other professional choices, was repeating the course. During her first attempt she had become quite overwhelmed by all the course demands and had found herself skipping lectures in order to do the project, and copying tutorial solutions. This year, with a lighter load of only doing a few courses, she was fully engaged with the course and enjoying it, especially as she was doing well. But she still had moments of panicking when she found she could not solve something and she had learned to walk away from things, relax and come back to it: 'when you're scared you can't do anything.'

Cyril was in a difficult situation. His first two years of chemical engineering had gone well but in his third year his father had become unemployed and so he had to take on part-time work to help support the family. He had struggled to find enough time for his work and had ended up failing most of his courses. The following year he again attempted them – alongside work in a retail store most evenings as well as helping with household chores – and had failed again.

The structural constraints of the chemical engineering curriculum do not easily allow for significant concurrent part-time work. This year was his third attempt to complete the third-year courses, and the advanced reactor engineering course was one of three that he was still carrying. He had been able to find work in one of the research groups within the department and felt confident that he was then managing to spend sufficient time on his academic work. He was also actively involved in his church. Strikingly, when asked to describe himself he said:

> If you ask me about myself, I'll start talking about family, first, and then my church work, my church stuff and probably after that I'll talk about chemical engineering, it probably definitely comes third, ja.

Here we have an expression of Cyril's emerging personal identity: chemical engineering is low on his list of concerns yet we know that this curriculum structure is incompatible with such a position.

Thus these four students start to paint a picture of the demands of the chemical engineering curriculum and the different ways in which they negotiate them, successfully or unsuccessfully. Students who were repeating the course said that their past failure was due to not finding sufficient time to meet these demands. Those who were 'on track' in the programme and doing the course for the first time were mostly having to dedicate every moment to keep on track. Across the class, this perception is widely shared: students speak of discipline and drudgery. They have become adept at dealing with a never-ending flow of tasks; the fulfilment relates to 'getting it done'. This is the structural reality of the chemical engineering curriculum. Students justify what they are going through in a sort of 'boot camp' mentality: if you can cope with this, you can cope with anything.

For these students the situation they found themselves in was one where the heavy demands of the course required them to fully prioritise the one project of academic success. Many of them dealt with this by attempting to deny their natural and full social well-being. They tried to spend every available minute on their studies. However, many students found that they simply were not able to continue pushing themselves at the extreme level that was required in the programme, and quickly came face to face with the academic consequences of slacking off. The prevalence of disengagement seemed to become more marked as the course progressed and students simply found themselves exhausted. In terms of dealing with the possibilities of connecting with peers and activities outside of the chemical engineering programme, many students felt they needed to say no to extra-mural activities and social invitations, and to keep themselves out of serious relationships. The cultural conditioning of the space of engineering education through its structural links to the external world of engineering work are seen in students who have taken on the perspective that this is most probably a good preparation for life after university. To explore this in more detail, we now consider the narratives of several more students in Sizwe's class: Rajesh, Sibongile and Peter.

Rajesh came to UCT having completed A-levels in his home country, an island off the east coast of Africa. He enjoyed chemistry at school and decided on that basis to do chemical engineering, although he said he did not know it would be 'such a mission'. He came from a small conservative community and revelled in the freedom of being at UCT: 'It was really nice getting from away from the home, doing what I could do and nobody watching my back.'

He passed first year with little effort, which was not surprising since South African first-year university courses are considered to be at A-level standard: 'Because I passed everything in my first year I thought like I didn't need to study much and I would pass and then things started going wrong, like badly.'

He ended up taking two years over the second-year courses, and was now on his second attempt at the third-year courses. He felt he had struggled with making the adjustment from a family life where his studying was closely watched and disciplined to having to take responsibility himself. He said: 'If my parents were here I'm sure I would have done my degree in my due time but, I mean, I'm not a very responsible person on my own.'

He felt that he had made the transition to being independent, and now he actually struggled when spending time back home, 'to get used to all these people around you'. But by third year he still felt that he had too many bad habits that he was trying to get rid of, 'to straighten out my life'. He had not got into a habit of studying regularly and typically would try and cram before the exams, which was often not successful. In responding to a question on why he had persisted he stated the following: 'I'm here to get my degree, though, I mean it was always my plan that I just, I didn't take the straight path, I've just been taking a long way road to get here.'

At the beginning of the previous year, life had changed radically when Rajesh was diagnosed with a serious illness. He had to go for a lengthy series of treatments. A bodily experience like this is a structural change of the first order, not something that can be reinterpreted or wished away but which needs to be faced head on. This experience seemed to coincide with some degree of a change in his approach to life and to studying. Like Phumzile, whom he worked alongside in class, he spoke of his ongoing difficulties to feel confident. He felt it was his central difficulty, and the repeated experience of failure had really knocked his confidence. When asked about the value of what he is doing, he says: 'It sort of like taught me about life, about how hard life is and what you have to go through.'

For Rajesh, then, it can be seen that coming to terms with the demands of the chemical engineering 'project' was a long and difficult process. Because he had succeeded in his first year with little attention to that project, he had been able to set up his life at UCT focused on socialising with little attention on the development of any ultimate concerns. At the time of the interview he was still struggling to refocus on that project, and put sufficient time and effort into his studies.

As noted in the introduction to this book, Sizwe's ability and determination to stay involved in a broader set of connections on campus was not the norm. Yet there were a few other students who also strongly asserted the importance of outside activities and connections. For some students it was involvement in church, which, for Sibongile, one of the top students in the class, involved meetings, leadership activities and many opportunities to meet new people. The first thing that Sibongile said about herself was that she was a Christian; this was something that she had taken on since coming to UCT. Going to church and church activities was a significant project in her life. She also prioritised friends and going to the movies – with a significant challenge to fit in the half-price movie evening with her study schedule – this was also an interest she had developed while at UCT.

Sibongile came from a small village in the northern part of the country. She had decided to do engineering since it was a route to get a bursary to fund one's studies. Of all the branches of engineering, the only one that attracted her was chemical engineering, because she had enjoyed chemistry at school. She had obtained a prestigious bursary from a multinational mining company, and had chosen UCT because it was far from home and she felt that would accrue status, coming back home and being from Cape Town. With hindsight she did not feel this was a 'valid reason' but she also said she did not regret her choice. Like Sizwe, she had entered chemical engineering through the ASPECT programme, a structured five-year programme intended to assist students who might struggle with the regular programme owing to their school backgrounds. She had performed well in the programme, and at the time of the interview was on track, having passed all her courses. She described herself as a hard worker:

> You know, chemical engineering is hard, and so, as a chemical engineering student I guess I can say that I work hard you know . . . for me to be doing 3rd year I guess I have to have worked harder, to get to this position here.

However, in talking about personal growth, Sibongile felt she had changed substantially as a person while at university, which she credited to her involvement in outside activities. She felt that her church involvement had helped her become a more reflective and open person. In chemical engineering, she said, there was no personal growth; 'it doesn't concentrate on you as a person'. It was her broader involvement at UCT which she found exciting: 'Coming here and meeting all these people from different backgrounds, different languages and different beliefs, it's challenging and exciting at the same time.'

Sibongile, it can be seen, managed to balance the 'chem eng' project alongside other interests quite successfully. The time she spent on her studies was productive – in due course we will take a closer look at this – and the other activities she engaged in seemed to have congruence with the demands of her study (no late nights, hangovers, etc.). She has an emerging personal identity in which her concern for a broader personal development could be accommodated alongside her concern to succeed academically. It is worth noting that both Sibongile and Sizwe were students who had been handpicked by industry, had achieved well at school and had gone through the ASPECT programme (presumably on advice of their bursars), which during the first year has a greater focus on the individual student and on personal growth than the regular programme.

Peter's dad was a chartered accountant, and he said, 'I just thought I'd try something different, and I kind of liked the sound of engineering and being an engineer.' But he knew he did not want to be a civil engineer, having seen through his father's colleagues and his sister's boyfriend that this involved a lot of moving around. He chatted to a lot of people, including a week's work shadowing at a sugar refinery, and 'the basic feel I got was that you can do the most with chemical engineering without having to make up your mind that that's what career you want to go into'. His parents, who were paying for his studies, encouraged him to go to Cape Town after they had seen how much his older sister had benefited from being away from home in Durban.

As it turned out, Peter really enjoyed having this responsibility for himself: 'I'm living my own life, I come and go as I please.' He did, though, confess: 'I probably worked a lot better at home than I do now.' He described himself as 'carefree' and said he did not like to do time management, although he had had to do this at the start of third year.

Peter thus felt that studying chemical engineering was a severe intrusion into his life:

> It takes up too much of my time and that, I think the Department sees us as chemical engineers who, and that's the only life we lead. And there's so much more that we do outside, and the minute I'm not at lectures I try to do as much as I possibly can outside of chemical engineering to like get away from it. But I think there's just too much expected of us or they just assume that we all love chemical engineering or it's really what we want to do or like, yeah.

He was worried about what he described as a lack of motivation; he felt he did not enjoy chemical engineering enough to do more than was needed to pass his courses – here he is grappling with balancing up what matters to him and noting that his studies are maybe not engaging him as much as he thinks they should. During his first year Peter felt that 'they spend a lot of time on us as people rather than chemical engineers. . . . But now they kind of think we're just chemical engineers and all those things that we spent discovering and like making new friends and doing new things, I think it's just kind of forgotten.' He did concede that now in third year he was able to handle much more work than he could in first year.

In summary

In this chapter we began to respond to the second central concern of engineering educators outlined earlier, namely the relatively low graduation rates of those who do enter the programme, particularly marked in the Anglophone world (the situation is quite different in engineering programmes in South East Asia). Existing work is largely focused on quantifying the 'pipeline' and the loss of students along the way. A social realist perspective notes the paucity of a model that does not have real individuals with real intentionality at its centre. Thus we need to engage with how the individual experiences engineering studies.

These vivid impressions have catapulted us into the world of what it feels like to be studying engineering. 'Project chem eng' is a project with structural constraints that demand from most students a near exclusive focus. This, for many students, clashes with their emerging personal identity, in which they want to see themselves as people who are not totally defined by their studies. Those who are putting a full focus on their studies, like Susan, feel resentful of this. A small group, including Peter and Sibongile, seem to balance sufficient academic work alongside other interests, like sport or church, that are important to them. Others have already suffered the consequences of not putting sufficient focus on their academic studies. Rajesh attempted a student life with lots of partying – away from the strictures of his family – and has already repeated multiple academic years. Now a serious health intervention has changed his perception of what matters to him in life, and he is attempting to shift the balance more towards his studies. Cyril has suffered the impact of a changing financial situation in his family – a massive structural change – and has to work part-time. This has taken its toll on his academic progress. It has also coincided with an emerging personal identity where there are other concerns like church that are much more important to him than his chemical engineering studies.

How do we proceed from this point? A simple response might be to say that studying is not meant to be fun. Maybe it is a good thing that these young people are being forced through a demanding curriculum to spend most of their time on academic work. To even start to unpack this social situation we need to interrogate the student learning experience more closely, both with regard to students' interactions with peers, as well as their engagement with knowledge.

Chapter 11

Studying engineering

Engaging with others

'No man is an island.' Contemporary educational literature emphasises the significance of the social context for learning. How does this work out practically in this demanding programme? What does it mean if a student fails to build peer networks? The narrative analysis in this chapter responds to these questions.

The social context for learning

The significance of the social context for learning is a contemporary theme in education research, signalled in the late 1970s with the rising popularity of the earlier work of the Russian psychologist Lev Vygotsky, who argued that higher mental functioning has a social origin: ideas that are first encountered in the social context are later internalised by the individual (Leach & Scott 2003). This is a perspective that sees a central significance for language in facilitating learning in the individual. The work of Vygotsky also provides a framework for thinking about how working alongside a more expert person can facilitate a child's learning in what he termed the 'zone of proximal development'. Thus we have the emergence of 'socio-cultural' perspectives on learning, emphasising discourse and participation (Sfard 1998), and these continue to be influential across education scholarship.

Researching student engagement in higher education

In a more applied sense this socio-cultural orientation spread into research on higher education, most notably through the research in the USA of Vincent Tinto and colleagues who showed that the more socially integrated students are into university communities of peers, faculty and staff, the more likely they are to persist in their studies (Tinto 1993). Another important applied line of research, especially prominent in engineering education reform in the USA, has been the development of teaching models to facilitate what has been termed 'collaborative learning' (Johnson et al. 1991). Numerous studies have shown increased student motivation as well as enhanced academic outcomes in teaching contexts where they are required to collaborate with their peers (Smith et al. 2005). Other innovations have focused on using peers in formal instruction and have shown empirical evidence to support this practice (Crouch & Mazur 2001).

Student engagement is now the buzzword of the new century. In the USA the National Survey on Student Engagement (NSSE) delivers scores that are closely interrogated by university managers and the broader public; an Australian equivalent plays a similar role (Kuh 2003; Hagel et al. 2011). We want students to engage with their peers and with their lecturers; we want them to feel part of a community. This is an increasing challenge in those contexts where many students have to do part-time work to fund their studies.

Moving towards a social realist approach

How do we figure engagement into a social realist approach to conceptualising student learning? Of course, it is human interaction that is at the centre of Archer's model of the morphogenesis of agency, and thus we should not be surprised at the significance of the social context for learning. Indeed, what the social realist approach has been offering throughout is a critique of any view on learning that confines itself to the individual learner.

Archer's concept of personal identity has been useful in the previous chapter for an initial analysis of students' experiences of learning, and now alongside this is placed the emergent *social identity*, introduced earlier in Chapter 7 (specifically on pp. 60–61). Social identity develops in a dialectal relationship with personal identity, and in the first instance points to two 'plural identities' that are emergent: *primary agency*, resulting from the circumstances of one's birth, which allies one's life chances with a demographic set of others; and *corporate agency* emerges when we band together with others in an attempt to collectively accomplish things in an organised mode that we cannot do individually. In contrast to these two group identities, a further development in the realm of social identity is held by the individual: the emergence of the *social actor*. This is a person who is able to 'personify' a social role in a distinct manner – expressive of their personal identity, that is, a reflection of what they care about most.

Student narratives of engagement with others

Students are in the process of developing a nascent personal identity, this identity being defined by a sense of what they care about and what they want to achieve. We obtained a small sense of some of the variation in that regard in the previous chapters when while still at school these young people chose to study engineering. Now they are third-year students. They are in the role of 'engineering students', but they might not as yet come to having personified this role in a manner that expresses their concerns and interests. They have landed up in a situation that has enormous structural constraints by virtue of the demands of the engineering curriculum. By definition they need to prioritise to succeed in the project of getting a degree. Many of them, as we saw above, have determined that in order to succeed in this project, they will need to suppress their other needs and desires. However, Archer notes that by virtue of our human constitution, it is not feasible to pursue only a sole project. Some students are finding that out as they start to show various manifestations of distress and depression.

It is all too true that agents can misjudge the costs that will be associated with a particular course of action. This is almost inevitable since we never make our deliberations in the presence of full knowledge of all the alternatives. Here we see a set of students who have embarked on a particular joined path, and for each of them this major 'project' is a result of internal deliberations about what they care about and what they hope to realise in their lives. In various ways they are now bumping up against the structural constraints in this situation. Archer describes this as a point where 'the nascent social identity impacts upon the nascent personal identity' (2000: 291).

What are the possible courses of action? In Sizwe's story and in a small number of his classmates we see students who are managing to sustain a *modus vivendi* that is not focused on the one project of succeeding academically at the cost of all others. They have a life 'outside chem eng', and they seem to maintain an extraordinary balance. These students are starting to build a social identity that defines differently the role of being an engineering student. Sizwe we can certainly cast in Archer's terms as a social actor, one who is able to forge a strong social identity from which one is able to provide leadership towards changing society. For the majority of the students in the class, though, there is an attempt to keep fully focused on the one project. Notably, there are ways of tackling this project that involve social engagements with one's classmates, and herein lies an important set of strategies.

Much discussion in engineering education seems to cast students as primary agents, defined by the circumstances of their birth context as advantaged/disadvantaged, black/white, middle class/working class, and so on. In the ways that lecturers interact with students these categories are often invoked (Smit 2012b), and thus many students further internalise their primary agency. To escape these circumstances requires the forging of corporate agency, and many students in the highly constrained environment of the engineering programme successfully forge strong peer bonds, which they can use towards achieving their own individual academic success.

We also need to explore the interactions that take place between the lecturer and the student. This relation is structurally defined as one with a clear power relation, but both students and lecturers are able to negotiate positions within that space. At the end of the day it is the lecturer that will make a judgement on the student's academic success, yet to differing degrees lecturers through their pedagogy will be able to work to facilitate that success. In different ways too, students will be able to navigate the relation with the lecturer towards obtaining what they need in order to succeed.

We now return to Sizwe's class to take a closer look at the range of ways in which peer and lecturer relations are negotiated and managed by individual

Table 11.1 Biographical details of students in Chapter 11

	Grew up in	Brought up by	Schooled at	Funding for studies
Sizwe	township	orphaned in high school, becomes child head of family	township state school	bursary
Phumzile	township	mother (father deceased)	low-fee private church school	bursary
Susan	suburb	mother and father	traditional private school	parents
Cyril	lower middle-class suburb	mother and father	multiracial state school	parents
Rajesh	foreign African country	mother and father	selective public school, completed A-levels	parents
Sibongile	rural area	parents divorced in high school, lives with father	rural state boarding school	bursary
Peter	suburb	mother and father	multiracial state school	parents
Andrew	suburb	parents divorced in primary school, lives with father	traditional private boarding school	parents
John	smallholding outside city	mother and father	traditional private boarding school	parents
Nkosazana	township	mother (father deceased)	rural state boarding school	bursary
Mcebisi	rural area	grandmother	rural state school	bursary
Tshepo	township	mother and father	low-fee private church school	bursary

students. As previously, this begins with the students who have already been introduced and thereafter further students are brought into the picture. Biographical details of this full group are given in Table 11.1. Many students in the class had a clearly defined small group of students that they worked with at least in the tutorials, and outside of class as well. These were often but not always the people that they sat next to in the lectures. For most students the group they worked with was a very small and racially homogeneous group, ranging from two to five people. Susan, with Peter and two other male students, Andrew and John, formed a close-knit group of four who not only worked together in class but were close friends outside class, going on holiday together, and so on. Peter spoke in some detail about this. He noted that the class was 'in little groups' and felt bad that he could not name everyone in class. Yet he found that others seem to find him approachable – 'more people know me than I know them' – and found that he could easily chat with them.

Andrew, who shared a flat with Peter, had attended a private boarding school and decided that he did not see himself moving back home and thus chose UCT, opting for chemical over mechanical engineering because he felt it had the 'greatest scope'. Andrew also spoke about their close friendship group and how it might be perceived in class:

I'm part of sort of quite a close group of friends in my class. In first year there were five of us who we started together, and we became like very close friends, because we all lived in residence on lower campus, so we became very good friends, and I think we've become a bit exclusive. I get on with the others in my class, and starting to get to know a lot of them better, but I still . . ., like, everyone's kind of formed their groups and I think because we're a circle I think it's quite hard for other people to break in, and I'm starting to notice it now more, and I think it's probably a little bit more difficult for other people to break into our circle because we've become such good friends.

He had thought about trying to build other connections in class but noted that this could be complicated:

There are a few groups, and I think it would be harder for me – I can get on with people – but I think it would be quite hard for me to sort of move, I mean because everyone sort of sits in there in their groups, [. . .] it wouldn't be very easy if I just all of a sudden just like moved and sat sort of three rows forward with a whole bunch of other people, partly because I don't know whether the others would accept me and then, the other thing there's my friends three rows back and I think they'll be a bit hectified [bothered] if I 'dis' [show disrespect to] them.

These four friends came from relatively similar social backgrounds; John had also been private school-educated. Of the four, he was the only one who at this stage in third year was feeling enthusiastic about chemical engineering. He felt that he was starting to see what the job would entail and he felt keen about that; he noted that his friends did not feel the same way; Susan actively said she did not want to be a chemical engineer, and Peter and Andrew were both a bit ambivalent. John felt that not everyone who chose chemical engineering was 'meant' to be a chemical engineer; the way he spoke about the profession was in the sense of a calling: 'You have to be quite a special person who's a chemical engineer.' At this stage he hadn't failed any courses and hoped to keep it like that, noting that Peter had failed one third-year course and Andrew had failed two.

Peter and Andrew, living in the same flat, had frequent connections while studying, popping into each other's rooms if they had a query. John said that he found it too distracting to try and actually study in the group of four, but that he would sometimes work paired up with either Susan or Peter. Thus we can see that these close friendships played a crucial role in these students' academic endeavours. In that this allowed a mediation of the challenges that the curriculum presented, we can consider this evidence of corporate agency. In this group we have noted that the corporate agents were a group who had shared primary agency.

The lecture theatre where the course lectures took place had two aisles dividing the class into three sections. Susan, Andrew, Peter and John sat in a row in the centre middle part of the lecture theatre. In the two rows in front of them sat the remaining seven white students in class, forming a distinct visual impression, given especially that two of these seven students dominated the question-asking in class. But in the very front row sat Sizwe with his two friends, and Sizwe's confidence in connecting with the lecturer and the class provided some counterbalance.

Across on the left-hand part of the class, also in the front row, sat Sibongile and her good friend Nkosazana. Like Sibongile, Nkosazana had also attended a boarding school. She had also chosen chemical engineering (over medicine) because she could obtain a sponsorship, was sponsored by the same mining company as Sibongile, and had also entered through the ASPECT programme. Over the four years these two had developed a very close friendship and could always be seen together. Nkosazana felt more conflicted than Sibongile about fitting in her academic work with the rest of her life. She felt that she had become 'less friendly' over her time in the programme, and felt this was not only because of the limited time available for socialising, but also because of how struggling academically had made her feel.

Nkosazana was one of the few students (together with Sizwe and the other two students mentioned earlier) who asked questions during the lectures. She thus came across as more confident and Sibongile as a bit more introverted, but both asserted the importance of being able to ask their classmates for help, and both said they felt they could approach anyone. Nkosazana described how she worked closely with Sibongile: 'She knows her stuff and she's very diligent; that's what I can say and I work well with her.' But she also asserted the importance of being able to approach others:

> I think it helps to work with other people because they give you direction, even with the project itself, I'll work in my room most of the time and then when I come up to the labs I realise that there's so much work that I haven't done. But when I was in my room I thought I was about to finish, you know, it's then they will like [say] 'Gee, Nkosazana, have you done this, have you done that?', I'm like, 'Oh my God, I didn't know that I had to go that deep into the project', like it helps to coordinate with other people, work with other people.

Thus we can note that Nkosazana and Sibongile represent another group of students who through their close relationships with each other exercise corporate agency in the face of the demands of the curriculum. In considering Susan and friends, Nkosazana and Sibongile, and Sizwe and his friends, though, we are looking at a small group of students who at this point in the programme had not repeated any years. They were still in class with the friends they had made in the junior years of the programme, and we have seen that some of these became very close friendships. Most of their immediate academic and social needs were met within this small group, but within these groups there was at least one student who spoke up in class and most of them were able to connect outside of their close friendship group to obtain help.

For most of the rest of the students in the class the situation was dramatically different, going through studies without a productive tight friendship group through which corporate agency could be exercised towards academic success. These students, without such a resource, found themselves frequently thrown back onto the limited resources of primary agency.

Cyril, Phumzile and Rajesh all spoke of the impact of repeating academic years on their ability to make social connections in the class. Cyril, who was doing part-time work, was not often seen in lectures, and when he did he sat in the back row along from Rajesh, who typically sat on his own. Rajesh worked with Phumzile in the tutorial, and said that apart from this he did not have any other connections in class. He said:

> All [my] good mates have already like graduated or been thrown out. I don't have time . . . like many friends here. . . . I find it pretty hard to talk to people in the chem eng department compared to other departments.

Cyril and Rajesh thus exemplify students who have little experience of corporate agency; who mostly mediate the constraints of the curriculum on their own.

Phumzile sat in the front row on the opposite side from Sibongile and Nkosazana. She had worked hard to feel part of this class. She described a number of occasions where she had struggled to feel accepted: not knowing where to sit and which group to join, asking a fellow student for clarification on an announcement and being told that the instruction was only for third years (which she was). But she had persisted and had built the ability to interact when needed with a fairly wide range of students in class. She described it thus:

> Even during the tuts [tutorials] you can see that these people want to work together but you can go there [and say], 'I don't understand this', at least they are willing to take a chair and say, 'Ah sit down with us'.

But she still wished for something more. She reflected on a module in the first-year courses that had focused on building group interactions, and she said, 'Maybe if we had like something like that, where we could just talk and get to know each other.'

Sitting in the same part of the lecture theatre as Phumzile were all male students, mainly students who had also come through the ASPECT programme, and who were mostly at least a year behind on their scheduled academic programme. In this group was Mcebisi, who came from a rural village in the northern part of the country with no running water or electricity and had attended the local school. There had been frequent teacher strikes throughout his school career, and in his final year of school there had been no teachers for most of the year. The students had to prepare by themselves for the final school examination, and Mcebisi had been one of only four students in the school who had received the level of results qualifying them for admission to university. His dream had been to study medicine, but when he heard of the marks needed for chemical engineering, as well as the possibility of sponsorship, he changed plans. He said he struggled with coming to UCT, and largely ascribed this to his difficulty in communicating in English; after five years at UCT he still said he did not feel confident in English. He struggled with a stutter and spoke very fast. The demands of university were also a huge shock to him. He felt he was being pushed – 'They wanted us to keep on working all the time' – through the whole semester. He had entered through the ASPECT programme and had struggled, falling a year behind in that programme. He said:

> This is like my fifth year here, I've seen people come and go. All my friends have got degrees at the moment and I'm like still not even being close to being able to get a degree.

He struggled to make good use of the formal class times. In the lectures he was annoyed by the one student who asked a lot of questions and seemed to monopolise the lecturer's time; he found this distracting. In tutorials he often left early and went home to his residence room. He preferred to seek out help on his own and had a wide range of people in the department that he felt comfortable consulting, including a number of graduate students. Thus Mcebisi had his own means for exercising corporate agency, through these connections, but these were temporary connections, which always required him to initiate them. He did not have ongoing sustained academic connections in the class. He was frustrated by his erratic academic performance and did not seem to know what worked for him; in many courses he would go from good marks in one test to a dismal fail in the next. When a test had gone poorly he would feel demotivated and struggle to pick himself up and work again.

Mcebisi described himself as outgoing and talkative. He felt confident to approach anyone in class. However, about some of the students in the class he said: 'They are not open to talking to other people, they want to keep to themselves all the time. Then when I meet them in the street like around Rondebosch then they won't say hi to me.' This really distressed him, and he described how he had to try and shut away this kind of experience and move on. His close connections were the other students who had come in with him through the ASPECT programme five years ago: Tshepo and two other male students. He shared a room in residence with Tshepo.

Tshepo came from a township outside a big urban centre and had attended a Catholic school there, which was considered to offer a very high standard of education in comparison to the other schools in the township. A large mining company came and did bursary interviews at his school; he was doing well in mathematics and science and had decided to do engineering but was not sure which branch. He chose chemical engineering because he was good at chemistry, but now thought he should have chosen mechanical engineering because chemical engineering had turned out to be what seemed to him to be a much tougher degree. Had he chosen mechanical engineering he felt he would already have graduated; as it turned out, like Mcebisi, he entered through ASPECT and was now in the fifth year of his studies but still at least another year away from graduation. When asked if he enjoyed doing chemical engineering, he said he was not exactly ecstatic: 'If you compare my attitude towards chemical engineering in first year or maybe when I was in matric to now, well it's changed, it's changed I promise you.'

He described the changes within himself as follows:

> I'd say I used to be very energetic about things you know, very excited, used to get excited about things. If there's a party this weekend – yeah! I've got a new girlfriend – hey! You know all those sorts of things, but now it's I don't get as much, there's a party this weekend – OK [said in low tone]. I've got to study for my test – OK [low tone]. You know. I guess it comes with being here for a while. It just sort of, I'm not out there anymore.

On the other hand, Tshepo thought that part of this might just be a maturing, moving from being very impulsive to be more considered in his actions. He felt it was useful to have become a bit more of an introvert, and he thought he needed to do this more, to keep more to himself. It had been really difficult to fall a year behind in the programme: 'I was supposed to be graduating this year, so I haven't exactly felt part of this current class.'

He was repeating the course and felt that that was because he had been insufficiently involved the first time around. This time he was really applying himself: 'I'm not taking it sitting down this time, I'm trying to get involved, I'm trying to pull myself through this.'

He described the advanced reactor engineering course as follows:

> I think it's a very involved course, you know . . . you need to spend much time outside lectures doing work on your own and you need to do a lot of it. You know you need to spend much time working it out, you need to attend tutorials, it's a very involved course.

Tshepo felt that his original class (now mostly in final year) had 'gelled' together well, but that this class tended to split into little groups. Social interaction outside of the class tended to be within these groups, and he wished that it was not so:

> It would be nice to have guys interacting with each other in the class. Do I think they can be changed? Definitely. How? That's the 'how' part I'm going to have a problem with. But yeah, I do think it can be changed.

Like Mcebisi, then, Tshepo missed the network of students with which he had been able to act corporately in his previous class. He made some connections, but these were insufficiently sustained to be a strong resource in his learning. Thus the crucial activity of using a peer network towards achieving academic success is very much constrained by the resources and knowledge that exist within the small group where a student finds him or herself. The broader peer resources of the class are not openly available except for the most confident.

In Tshepo's narrative, though, we see the impact of another very crucial social relation, that with the lecturer. Tshepo noted that the way the lecturer interacted with them made a huge difference to his learning. He described it thus:

> The Prof himself he gets us involved in class. You tend to grasp things more by just listening to him and understanding what he says in class, asking questions than just by studying yourself. I mean I could always study myself, but his methods of teaching, he doesn't just take everything from the textbook. You need to be involved in the class, you need to concentrate more, I mean. If you come to class and don't concentrate it's like sort of not coming to class at all. So I try to come to class each time and try to, you know, concentrate. He asks questions, solve this and then he goes around. This is the type of thing I come to class for. It's the small things that help, they really help.

He also spoke at length about the value of the tutorial, particularly because of the opportunity to get further contact with and explanations from the lecturer. Interactions with the lecturer similarly take place within a social context that is differentially navigable by individual students. This lecturer was at particular pains to treat all students equally and had a strong commitment towards facilitating success for students from disadvantaged backgrounds. Given the structure of the lecturer–student power relation, it would appear that this intention had a relatively significant effect on recrafting the space. A number of other students also spoke in detail about the lecturer's mode of interacting with students in the lecture theatre: he would give students a problem to work on and walk around in the lecture theatre and discuss with individuals the approach they were using. Andrew said the following about this experience:

> He explains things really well and he makes sure that you understand things in the lectures, like the way he'll start off like say an energy balance and make you finish it, so you sit there and all of a sudden you have to do something and then he walks around and checks them and you know even if you don't do anything he'll come past, he'll see that you haven't done anything and he'll ask you what you think you're going to do, and I mean just having to think about it for those few minutes it just, I mean, cause you could sit there through the lecture and just blankly stare at the board, maybe write down notes, but it doesn't really sink in unless you actually give it some thought and he makes you think about it when it's happening, it's important, because other courses like you get all the information, you get to the tuts and then you've got to go back sort of [by a] few weeks' lectures and try and remember what was said and little bits that you haven't . . ., that you've missed.

Quite a few students consulted the lecturer either in their small groups or one-on-one both after the lecture and in his office. Many students felt that this was something exceptional about this particular lecturer, and for some this was their first experience of actually engaging with a lecturer at all. Indeed, when describing why they felt this was a particularly good lecturer, which many students did, this aspect was often mentioned, along with the quality of his explanations. Mcebisi said he had consulted this lecturer twice in his office during the semester and said he was very helpful, gave good explanations and made you feel you could 'make it'.

When asked about what hindered or facilitated his learning on this course, Sizwe said the following, summing much of significance in this chapter:

> Other students and the easy access of [the lecturer] facilitated my learning in the course because I mean he was I mean [the lecturer] himself was part of the motivation that I do extra work late, I mean on my own. And obviously the assistance that you get from students as well was very important.

How can we characterise this lecturer's actions in terms of Archer's theory? Clearly, the interactions with the lecturer were quite central to students' engagements with the knowledge in this course. These went well beyond good explanations, but in many actions noted here it can be seen that the lecturer made deliberate interventions to facilitate and promote student learning. In this very specific personification of the role of lecturer, so closely and deeply linked to the knowledge in this course, we can characterise the lecturer as a social actor.[1]

In summary

This chapter continued the exploration of the student experience of learning, focusing here on engaging with peers and lecturers. It was noted that 'socio-cultural' perspectives on learning have grown in prominence in recent times. There is also a great deal of quantitative research that argues for the importance of student 'engagement' in facilitating student academic success. Moving towards a social realist approach, we draw on a stratified model of identity, comprising both personal and social identity.

This chapter has developed a description of the interactions that characterise the experience of engineering education for individual students. We have noted the significance of corporate agency where groups of students worked together to enhance their chances of academic success. For students who were academically 'on track', most seemed to have developed tight friendship groups that sustained them both socially and academically. Here we noted the group of white students constituting Susan and her friends as well as the close pair of Sibongile and Nkosazana.

For students who had fallen behind academically, a devastating consequence had been the difficulty of building networks in a 'new class'. Across these narratives we did not note any instance of success in building a new network. These students seemed thrown back completely on their individual resources – even to initiate contacts for help – and occasionally on the apparent presence of a demographic group marked by primary agency – for example, black students from poor school backgrounds. Cyril came into class from his part-time work and left again with minimal contact except that he usually sat next to Rajesh. Rajesh worked with Phumzile in the afternoon tutorials (Cyril seemed to have been exempted from these), and said that he did not have any contacts in the class. Mcebisi and Tshepo were friends and also started in the same intake, but this friendship did not translate into productive corporate agency towards academic success or class engagement.

The social actor, as expected, is a rare achievement particularly among this age group, but in Sizwe and his personification of the role of class representative we have an exemplar of a social actor. He is seen encouraging his classmates to maintain a balance between their academic project and other things that are necessary for well-being and personal development.

The lecturer acts in a role whose objectives need to be understood as different from those of the students, although clearly interrelated (Ashwin 2009). There is of course a necessary relation between the roles of lecturer and student; a lecturer cannot exist without a student to teach, and, for the most part, being a student implies having lecturers who teach you. In the actions of this particular lecturer we noted a personification of the role in line with a personal identity structured around student success – this social actor stepped out of the regular confines of the role to engage with students and facilitate their learning. All students, and most especially those who were struggling, noted this lecturer's efforts to assist them to succeed. It was particularly evident that this lecturer made overt efforts to be available to all students regardless of background, and this seemed crucial to the impact of this role.

Earlier we noted these students who chose chemical engineering have found themselves on a highly constrained path. It requires a serious prioritisation of the one project, which is academic success, which can be straightforwardly defined as passing the various courses that comprise the degree. We now turn to a more in-depth examination of this 'knowledge project', that is, the acquisition of engineering knowledge, but bearing in mind the broader context in which this learning takes place, both the historical structural conditioning of the space, and the network of interactions in which the individual student participates.

Note

1 I am grateful to Kevin Williams for this insight.

Chapter 12

Studying engineering
The knowledge project

In the previous chapter we established that students who have chosen to study engineering are in a situation that requires them to significantly prioritise course demands over any other concerns. We have noted too that many engineering students attempt to suppress other projects at this time, sometimes to the detriment of their overall well-being, and ultimately of course to the detriment of their academic project. What does this academic project look like, termed here 'the knowledge project'? The engineering curriculum is a recontextualisation of engineering knowledge, and as such has a particular structure. What does it mean for learning in this knowledge area?

The significance of knowledge in science and engineering education research

In contemporary social realist scholarship there has been a strong focus on 'reclaiming knowledge' (see, for example, Muller 2000; Young 2008), which can be largely understood as a response to the influence of post-modernism in the humanities disciplines, which, in questioning the value of the 'canon', had a tendency to devalue knowledge as such. In science and engineering education it could be argued that the central importance of knowledge has never been under question. Early research, especially in science education, used cognitive psychology approaches centred on students' understandings of core science concepts (see, for example, Pfundt & Duit 1994; Nakhleh 1992). Based on constructivist learning theory, which focuses on the individual student building understanding of core concepts, theories of conceptual change were developed as well as associated pedagogies (Posner et al. 1982). Current work in engineering education continues to focus, for example, on identifying 'threshold concepts' to enable the development of conceptual understanding (for example, Park & Light 2009).

Another influential line of work in higher education, mentioned briefly in the Introduction, focuses on 'approaches to learning', which describe students' intentions while studying; these are understood as responses to their perceptions of the educational context. 'Deep' approaches describe students who direct their work towards developing understanding, while 'surface' approaches are a minimal response directed towards course and assessment demands, at the expense of understanding (Case & Marshall 2009). In earlier work we identified a third approach prevalent in science and engineering, the 'procedural' approach, in which students focus on solving problems – with 'deep procedural' towards an ultimate goal of understanding, and 'surface procedural' towards memorising of standard solutions (Case & Marshall 2004). A study of second-year chemical engineering students at UCT showed that the time-pressured course context resulted in students struggling to make the required shift towards a deep approach to learning (Case & Gunstone 2003).

Moving to a social realist approach

Knowledge – in all its forms – is one of the most significant personal emergent properties that humans possess. Archer identifies just two other crucial such properties: self-consciousness and reflexivity. Self-consciousness, as noted, is something we acquire in early childhood and remains a requirement for maintaining a normal psychological life. In the context of higher education we can generally assume that this personal property is in place; in cases where it is fractured it will require the professional input of the psychologist rather than the educator. We have noted how reflexivity is central to the ability to identify a substantial project, and we note that in order to succeed in engineering it will require a serious prioritisation of this project. In this chapter we need to move closer into examining what it is to acquire knowledge in engineering.

Acquiring knowledge involves a specialisation of consciousness, building a new way of looking at the world, a *gaze* (see discussion on p. 55). This has some resonances with the work of Roger Säljo on 'conceptions of learning', in which the most inclusive conception includes all of acquiring information, making meaning, applying knowledge to problems and, significantly, taking on a new perspective. In Archerian terms we are talking about the morphogenesis of agency. This is not an easy process, for at least two key reasons. As the work of James Gee makes so clear, taking on a new identity can be very hard if it clashes with an existing identity that you hold dear. In Archer's terms we would consider this the difficulty of pursuing projects that have divergent aims. Second, the specialised gaze does not come easily; it involves not only the ability to 'recognise' the knowledge practices in this new domain, but also the ability to 'realise' one's own legitimate products. In much of higher education, the specialised knowledge practices have precursors in the discourse of the middle-class home, and thus for some students it is much easier to build this gaze than it is for others.

Framing this process in terms of a *morphogenetic cycle* (see Chapter 4, specifically pp. 47–49), we can see that the acquisition of knowledge takes place in the context of social and socio-cultural interaction, a context that is heavily conditioned by structural and cultural antecedents, and a space in which individuals weigh up their concerns and decide on a course of action. We need to develop a fuller understanding of engineering education as an education system. We need to figure out how pedagogy and curriculum come together to structure the space in which students 'learn', and we need to see how this relates to the broader context of the university and to the world of work. It has already been noted in Chapter 8 that the curriculum can be considered as the ultimate manifestation of the structural and cultural conditioning of the space of engineering education. It represents the accommodation between the interests of the academy and those of the world of practice – with a programme that moves from basic science in the first year, through to engineering science, and then to project-based work in the senior years.

With regard to researching student learning in engineering from a social realist approach, Kotta's (2011) PhD study is significant. Here she closely followed a class of third-year chemical engineering students in their first major design course, then followed the same students going into their fourth year, culminating in the capstone 'design project'. She shows how learning to produce legitimate text in design requires a quite different set of capacities from those that have been honed in the engineering sciences courses. Here students are once again operating under stringent time pressure. The task requires them to utilise their prior knowledge, which of course will pose some challenges if they have been managing to scrape through by solving examination problems without real understanding. But perhaps more crucially, design requires them to make decisions about how to spend their time, about what computer tools to use, at what stage to 'freeze' the design and start writing up, on how to use (often sketchy) feedback that the lecturer has provided, and which friends to choose to consult for advice. Kotta's study shows how some students were able to exercise their personal emergent properties in such a way as to achieve success in design, but how others were not able to navigate the constraints of this situation successfully. Importantly, compared to the explicit right/wrong context of problem-solving in the engineering science courses, the evaluative criteria (what would be considered by the marker to be a good design) were much more fuzzy, and lecturers were generally not successful in giving students a sufficiently explicit sense of what they were looking for. In some cases this was compounded by lecturers who did not manage to get promised interim feedback to students in time for them to correct their work before the final submission.

Kotta's study gives us important insights into how students make use of peer interactions towards achieving success in design. Crucially, she shows that even though most successful students made extensive use of peer input they were also able to withdraw from this group at important stages and make autonomous decisions on their work. The students who failed design were noted for their inability to exercise autonomy at any stage of the project. She shows how their prior experiences had led them to believe that chemical engineering was not something that they could succeed at on their own, and during the design project they only had this single strategy at hand. Disturbingly, these students' lack of self-confidence was compounded by the messages they received from their peers and from the way they experienced interactions with the lecturers.

Compared to Kotta's study, the present case study takes a step backwards in the engineering curriculum to the arena of an engineering science course, one of the precursors to the formal design course. Although this advanced reactor engineering course did include a small design project, the majority of the course was structured in the traditional mode through which engineering science is taught and delivered in engineering curricula around the world. The lecturers present theoretical ways in which the students need to learn to model real-world problems in reactor engineering, and then they need to demonstrate this in quantitative problem-solving in tutorials, tests and the final examination. Performance in these assessments is what determines passing or failing in this course. We move now to consider how students take on the challenge of progressing through this curriculum, specifically focusing on their engagements with the knowledge at hand.

Exploring the knowledge project through student narratives

In narratives of the third-year chemical engineering students in Sizwe's class we can see what the 'knowledge project' means for these students. At this stage we now add the final students to make up the group of 14 that comprise this case study. Their biographical details are summarised in Table 12.1. In their narratives we again see echoes of the deep/surface distinction in approaches to learning, with most students asserting the importance of focusing towards understanding (the deep approach). For example, Sibongile stressed that in this course one needed 'to understand and not just to go through the motions of doing the calculation'. She said that 'getting to understand' and 'knowing how to do it' are two distinctly different things. She said if you just knew how to do a problem without understanding what you were doing, then you would likely get stuck in a test when you were given a different problem to do. John stated outright: 'I don't like doing stuff without understanding it.' Peter was straightforward and said: 'I know how to pass courses rather than actually learn.' However, he did note that the advanced reactor engineering course was not the kind of course where he could 'get by with just learning how to do seven types of questions', and thus in this course he was focusing on the fundamentals.

A number of students felt that this course, which integrated material from earlier courses and pointed towards practical applications, was interesting because of its relevance to what they would be doing one day. Sizwe said: 'I think my experience with it made me feel more like an engineer, you know in practice.' Andrew said: 'It's been one of the more interesting courses we've done because it's more like every time we do something it's more and more relevant to actual engineering.' John said that in the first two years of the programme 'you're not really sure what exactly you're doing', but that in this course everything had started to come together: 'So it just started to make sense why we learnt this and why we learnt that.' Here we see clear evidence of how learning engineering has implications for

Table 12.1 Biographical details of students in Chapter 12

	Grew up in	*Brought up by*	*Schooled at*	*Funding for studies*
Sizwe	township	orphaned in high school, becomes child head of family	township state school	bursary
Phumzile	township	mother (father deceased)	low-fee private church school	bursary
Susan	suburb	mother and father	traditional private school	parents
Cyril	lower middle-class suburb	mother and father	multiracial state school	parents
Rajesh	foreign African country	mother and father	selective public school, completed A-levels	parents
Sibongile	rural area	parents divorced in high school, lives with father	rural state boarding school	bursary
Peter	suburb	mother and father	multiracial state school	parents
Andrew	suburb	parents divorced in primary school, lives with father	traditional private boarding school	parents
John	smallholding outside city	mother and father	traditional private boarding school	parents
Nkosazana	township	mother (father deceased)	rural state boarding school	bursary
Mcebisi	rural area	grandmother	rural state school	bursary
Tshepo	township	mother and father	low-fee private church school	bursary
Zanele	rural area	parents divorced in primary school, lives with father	rural state school	bursary
Mpho	township	grandmother	low-fee new private school	bursary

the emergent personal identity. If you are starting to feel that 'being an engineer' is going to be a sensible part of working through what matters for you, then this will be a significant positive impact on your learning in this course. This resonates with earlier work characterising student learning in the second year of the same programme (Case & Gunstone 2006).

Many students asserted the actions that helped in building understanding. Phumzile said that tackling problems in the tutorials rather than just copying down a solution really helped 'because you know if you're struggling with something you understand it better'. Many students asserted that the lectures helped build understanding, first because of the quality of the lecturer's explanations, but also because he forced them to tackle problems on their own in the lecture theatre, and would walk around and discuss their work with them. Andrew said of the lecturer: 'He makes you think about it when it's happening, it's important, because other courses like you get all the information [then when] you get to the tuts and then you've got to go back [a] few weeks [of] lectures and try and remember what was said.' These strategies that students found valuable link to much contemporary scholarship, which characterises such behaviours under the label of 'active learning' (see, for example, Johnson et al. 1991; Rosenthal 1995; von Blottnitz 2006).

In the previous chapter we have seen how peer networks were a crucial resource for students in this course, and that those who lacked such networks suffered a particular disadvantage. However, looking at this more closely in terms of how students use these networks the picture is a little more nuanced. For example, while asserting the value of his group of close friends, John pointed to the importance of working alone: 'You've got to have the time alone where you sort things out.' This position links to the earlier findings of Kotta (2011) mentioned above, who found that notwithstanding the significance of good peer networks, the individual student needed to build confidence in their own ability to produce legitimate course outputs.

Notwithstanding the central significance of building understanding, many students pointed out that this course required more than that. Sizwe said: 'I understand most of the material, ja, I understand most of the material. My only fear is that you can fail even if you understand.' Some students were able to elaborate on this challenge. The sheer volume of work and the complexity of the problems resulted in what Susan termed 'all these little things I need to know', and Rajesh described as 'little deviations and variations on the problem'. Tshepo said that he understood the material but had difficulty in implementing his understanding when trying to solve a problem. Sibongile spoke of the difficulty of pulling this all together under the pressure of the examination: 'You don't think properly to a point that you make a lot of mistakes.'

The difficulty on maintaining a focus on understanding under the course pressure was noted by Nkosazana. She said that at the start of the semester she was on top of everything and understanding the work, but as the semester progressed and she started to focus on the project, she found this focus slipping:

> There's so much work and the work is hard and you know like trying to keep up with the work at the same time understanding and you end up, let me just get through and then you know, I can get the understanding later and later never comes.

In an honest reflection she went on to express her concerns about the potential impact of not understanding this work for when she has to tackle the final-year design project:

> I think that the curriculum is over packed, it's too much to, at the end of the day you just pass but you don't know anything from it, and when you ask to apply it for your design next year, you find that you'll be surprised that you

can't even do mass balance while you've gone from first year to last year but you never got time to sit down and really get to understand the basics.

Compared to some of the others, aspects of Cyril's description of his approach seemed to indicate a degree of passivity. In response to an opening question on how things were in this course, he centres on 'having the notes': 'I've got the notes from previous years, all the notes is in the text book as well and he gives us the notes so, things seems to be going okay for now.' In another quote he talks about 'going through' and 'reading through', even though he does talk about 'understanding of what's going on':

> The textbook I find very helpful so I go through the textbook quite often, the tuts [are] also very helpful getting to grips with actually doing the examples helps with the understanding of what's going on as well, so I basically go through the tuts and I read through the textbooks mainly.

These reported behaviours are a striking contrast to the picture of active engagement noted above – with struggling with problems in tutorials, seeking out explanations for the concepts you struggle with, etc.

Some students were explicit about feeling lost. In working on the design project, Susan said that she had had a discussion with the lecturer at which point she felt she knew what was going on, but when working on the project again on her own, 'I kind of felt like I lost the whole picture and I'm a bit confused now.' She spoke about the difficulty of making progress on your own without assistance, something also echoed by Mcebisi:

> It looks easy when you're like sitting in class when the lecturer is presenting the whole thing to you. Like in the tuts you get around and you can see the aspects that he's trying to present to you. But then after all the help has been removed from me, there's no lecturer, there's no tutor and [I] say let me do this, I don't go anywhere, . . . by myself I can't go anywhere, I need someone to be with me, a tutor, someone to like guide me through.

In summary, then, looking through all the narratives to date we note the complexity of what successful learning in this knowledge area demands. Not only does it require the cumulative building of knowledge, but the pace that is set by this curriculum is demanding and the level of detail is substantial. Many students report on the behaviours that they know will lead to success in this course: it demands an active engagement, grappling with difficult concepts and problems, and independence even within the context of a strong peer network. This engagement also takes place within the wide process of needing to identify to some extent with the project of 'becoming an engineer'. On the other hand, we also note students who are not managing to pull this off. The time demands are substantial and if you fall behind you are really lost. There is some reporting of a relatively passive approach to work, which contrasts strikingly with the active engagement that many students report as essential for success.

To continue to explore these preliminary findings, we now turn to the detailed narratives of two further students in the class, Zanele and Mpho.

Like Mcebisi, Zanele had also grown up in a small village in the northern part of the country and had attended the local schools. She had wanted to be a doctor, but then she realised that bursaries were more readily available for engineering, and a teacher also encouraged her to do chemical engineering, given her good marks in mathematics and science. She chose UCT as she wanted to be far from home. When she arrived, the main shock was having to use English, and she was relieved to find a sub-warden in the residence with whom she could chat in Sesotho. But she had performed well academically, and was fully on track in the fourth year of the five-year ASPECT programme. She felt she had done well in the earlier years because the courses were 'more mathematical' – 'I know that I am good in calculation and that stuff' – but she was feeling less confident in the senior years of the programme, which involved more project-type work involving written reports and oral presentations. This had made her wonder whether she had chosen the wrong career.

She described herself as shy but had a small group of friends in the class. During the tutorials she worked closely with one of these, Mpho. However, she also felt sufficiently confident to go and ask others in the class for help if she needed it: 'If I have a problem and I see that this person is good and that then, ja, I can go and ask questions and everything.' Here we can see the independent focus on developing good understanding that was asserted by other students above as essential for success.

Zanele spoke in detail about how she went about studying in the advanced reactor engineering course. She had a clear sense of when she had mastered a topic, and usually referred to this in terms of 'understanding', although she also referred to mastery of problem techniques and algorithms. In discussing her learning in the course she frequently mentioned particular topics that she had grappled with, for example, here what she termed 'the catalyst thing(y)':

> Well, ja the catalyst thingy, I'm not confident about that one, I still have problems with the catalyst thing, but coming to the steady state thingy ja it's okay that, and the unsteady state then I can understand what's happening in there. Like what I've realised is that in Chapter 8 and 9 like all you need to do is to do the like to just to go from defining your conversion and do your mole balancing, your energy balance then you'll see from there what's the problem.

In talking about how she got to this point of mastery she particularly emphasised the value of the tutorials, mainly in terms of the explanations that the tutors gave. She appreciated that they did not just tell you how to solve the problem, but they explained the material so that you could proceed and solve it yourself. Where she had encountered a useful explanation she made notes for herself on it, which she termed 'additional notes', for example when the lecturer had explained a particular graph in class. She made the effort to attend most lectures and had noted the value of lectures when she missed one and found that she could not so easily understand the material working directly from the textbook.

She worked with her friends when as part of revising for a test they would go individually through past papers and then consult each other when stuck, but otherwise she asserted strongly the importance of studying on her own.

Thus with Zanele we see the strong reassertion of a range of approaches that other students had claimed as essential for success: independent although with peers to consult, strongly focused on understanding, consulting widely, checking and assessing her own understanding. One thing that she did not mention much was whether this course linked to any emerging sense of becoming an engineer.

Like Zanele, Mpho had entered through the ASPECT programme four years before, but she was carrying one of the core second-year courses alongside her third-year courses. She grew up in an urban township in the north-west of the country, was brought up by her grandmother, and for high school had attended a low-fee private high school in Johannesburg, one of those that focus on delivering good academic results but without a broader traditional school environment of private schools at the other end of the financial scale. Thereafter she was selected to be one of ten students in a bridging programme offered by a chemical company. Most of the graduates of this one-year programme had gone on to do diplomas at the technikon,[1] but Mpho had elected to go to UCT:

> I always wanted to do extra things, I also told myself that you know I'm an ordinary person, trying like to do extra things, where people do ordinary things and I always wanted to get a degree, not a diploma or something.

Failing tests and failing courses had been a really hard experience – 'I never knew what it was like to get low marks. . . . It used to depress me when my class tests were not okay, and even today I'm still not used to that.' She was in a serious relationship, and also found it hard to balance the emotional demands that this made on her alongside her academic requirements.

For Mpho it was really important to be able to connect with others: 'In most cases I always like confirming things before I do them.' She felt that it was not possible to figure out by yourself what to do in the course and that you needed others to help you. But in considering the options, she was quite explicit about some of the limitations in the class dynamics:

> I still see that there's a little bit of people dividing themselves in a sense of being black and white, it's difficult to like, when you have a problem to, . . . it's difficult to go to a for instance a white person and ask them like a question, but some of them it's easy to relate to them, like you can actually go and ask them and they can explain things, but some of them it's like you know, it's really difficult to talk to them.

She continued:

> Like there are only two white girls in my class, I find it easier to talk to them, like if we ask them things for the first time they not sulking or anything, they are free to open up and tell you things, and like in my prac group like we relate well together and there's a couple of us, black and white, and it's easy because they always say things and then if I don't understand I ask them, but there are others that, I don't know, it's just like that there's always gonna be something like that worldwide, [some] people want to be this side and that side.

She was particularly concerned knowing that the high-stakes final-year design project would be in randomly assigned groups:

> The other day I was telling my friends that next year when we do our design we'll be grouped, and when it's difficult for you to relate to a person, how are you going to . . . cause you'll find that sometimes in our class there are people that always wanna talk, they don't give other people chance to, ja and it becomes, I don't know, it makes you feel inferior again at times, at times it's overwhelming.

She contrasted this with the class ahead of her with whom she had shared some of the earlier courses (the ASPECT programme spreads the first two years over three years), and which she felt related better to each other, across the colour lines. Her religious faith had been a huge source of comfort to her through the challenges of failing academically, and she also drew from that a view of the intrinsic value of all people, which she felt contrasted with the arrogance of the students she felt were looking down on her:

> It's like there's no one who's wise and there's no one who's stupid, yes, and we have what it takes to make it through life and . . . people [who] thought they're like nothing, they're something.

She was trying to improve her self-discipline to focus on her work, to avoid, for example, switching on the TV and getting distracted from her studies. She felt that she hadn't worked sufficiently hard in previous years because she had felt she knew her work:

> I never used to worry a lot cause I thought I knew things, . . . that's why I used to play a lot, I used to work when it was needed.

Mpho really struggled with maintaining an even and consistent focus of effort across all her courses. When something interested her she found all her attention going in that direction; the advanced reactor engineering lecturer had presented the work in a manner that had really captured her interest. She was worried that she was not putting sufficient effort into her other courses. She also related this to the lecturer's punctuality and consistency: she remarked that his punctual appearance at 8am every morning inspired her to work harder. But she still struggled to have the consistent level of effort and interest that the course demanded:

> In most cases . . . like I have this interest of knowing what, like for instance if he talks about the catalyst then I'll get interested and I'll go after the lecture and then ask questions when I didn't understand clearly what he was saying. But sometimes when I'm tired . . . and sometimes you really are tired.

Right now the design project had captured all her attention. She was attending lectures but worrying about the project, especially if she had heard someone else talking about an aspect of the project that she hadn't tackled. She was aware of the need to work on her own on mastering the material from the lectures – what she describing as 'reading' (presumably over her notes and in the textbook) – and had not been doing this during the second half of the course when the project had taken over her focus:

> Like, for the things that we did, ever since after the vac[ation] now, I don't think I'm in track with them like, I still need to go and, I understood what he said in the lecture, but I think I need to study them in a sense like to read because I don't think I've been reading a lot ever since this project came.

She was all too aware that many times her focus was insufficient: 'With other courses sometimes I just do the tut and I don't feel that I've done the tut.' She felt the tutorials in this course were valuable, but strikingly noted: 'Even when I don't write things and I leave at five I understand what I'm doing and I sit down in my room.' Not writing down anything during the afternoon would be a definite limitation on what can learn in the context of these lengthy and challenging problems.

It was a difficult emotional experience all round. She found herself crying at her desk after sitting for hours trying to do the project on her own. She panicked in tests when something unexpected appeared on the test paper.

Crucially important was accessing people who could give good explanations, either in the lecture, in the tutorial, or informally:

> [The lecturer] explained so much that I tend to visualise, and it really helps because I can see what he's talking about, I can close my eyes and see what he really means when he says the diffusion inside the catalyst pore.

Mpho's experience alerts us strongly to the emotional dimension of the experience of learning. When things are happy and one is feeling connected to peers, it is easy to miss that there is much positive emotional benefit that is not necessarily recognised. Mpho's difficulties in feeling part of this class had a direct impact on her learning. Specifically, she struggled to mobilise the kind of focus that was needed for success in this course. She was not able to sufficiently direct effort across all the various parts of the course, and she often found herself in an emotional space that precluded productive work.

With an Archerian perspective we can note that the situational logics of the course environment have set up a defined range of options for students. With only very limited time at hand they need to decide strategically what course of action to pursue. Clearly, depending on their personal resources (in Archer's terms their 'personal emergent properties'), particular courses of action will be estimated to take up particular amounts of time. For a student who is struggling to understand the new concepts being presented it is quite understandable that they might well recognise that they do not have sufficient time available to be able to invest in developing conceptual understanding. What is going to matter in terms of the project of succeeding in the degree will be passing in the examination. A perusal of the examination will show that it comprises a number of quantitative problems, which on the face of it appear similar to those tackled in class and in the afternoon problem sessions. A logical response is to attempt, then, to internalise the problem-solving methods that can be applied to these problems. Where this approach falls short is that although on the face of it the problems might seem similar, the examination questions are structured in such a way that many of them really do test whether students understand the underlying concepts in this portion of chemical engineering science. The student who lacks this understanding will present a lot of quantitative working in their examination script but might well fail to obtain passing marks for their work. The structural constraint of extreme time pressure thus serves as a major constraint on student learning for many students in chemical engineering.

The hierarchical nature of the knowledge in question means that all parts of the course are deeply interrelated. Falling behind in the fundamentals will exact a toll across other parts of the course. The need to produce satisfactory solutions to examination problems means that just 'understanding' the concepts on its own will be insufficient to ensure a passing result.

At this point it is pertinent to consider the reported academic outcomes on this course. Mpho failed. So did Cyril. All the other students whose narratives have been presented earlier passed, while Susan was the only one to obtain a mark greater than 70 per cent. When compared to the overall class (who achieved a pass rate of 62 per cent), it can be seen that the group of students here are in fact a relatively successful subset of the class (with a pass rate for the group of 86 per cent). Some of this can be easily explained: the initial students who participated in the study were those who were present in the class and able to respond to the invitation to participate (all except three of these 39 students requested to participate); the 14 students whose narratives are used in this book are those who were first traced in the follow-up study (i.e. those with a visible career-based internet presence). Drawing on Flyvbjerg's (2001) typology of case studies, we can consider this a kind of 'best case' group – they are a generally successful group in this programme. If we observe any concerns about their experiences of the curriculum, then these would only extrapolate to larger concerns in the broader class, and especially so if considering the full intake to the programme.

In summary

At the outset of this chapter we noted that knowledge has always been a central focus in studies of student learning in science and engineering education. Working with a social realist perspective here, we have obtained new insights on these challenges. The importance of a deep approach to learning, which prioritises conceptual understanding, has been strongly underscored in this study. However, we also see other actions that are necessary to achieve academic success in this course, as noted both in what students themselves report as being important, as well as the observed outcomes of this group whose narratives have been featured. A range of behaviours that constitute active engagement are reported – grappling with problems, assessing one's own understanding and seeking out help. These contrast strongly with more passive accounts that prioritise things like 'having the notes'. Significantly, although these students value peer networks, for academic success they also recognise the need to independently manage their own learning. Some students do note the ways in which the relevance of the material in this course ties into their emerging identity as engineers, and this does appear to be a particular benefit to their learning – as would be expected with a congruence between these two personal projects.

The structural constraints of this curriculum have been noted. There is a tremendously large volume of work, both conceptually demanding but also with significant detail, that needs to be managed in a relatively short period of time. Success does not come without significant personal investment.

Note

1 South African term for institutions that offered two-year diplomas, largely vocational in orientation, similar to the UK 'polytechnic'. These institutions have now been designated 'universities of technology' and offer degrees.

Chapter 13

Conclusions for the case study

It is now ten years since these students were in third-year chemical engineering. What happened to them? This chapter draws on follow-up interviews to start the process of drawing together the conclusions of the case study.

Completing the narratives

The narratives of student learning that have been drawn on in this book derive from interviews that were conducted with students in a senior engineering course at UCT. Here we considered 14 students and presented narratives that started with their choice to study engineering and moved into their experience during this third-year course. Some ten years after this original study, telephonic follow-up interviews were conducted. At this point we can now complete the story, taking them through to graduation and then into their careers.

First, we need to consider the time to graduation. Table 13.1 shows for each student the number of years that they had been in the programme at the time they were taking the third-year course under investigation. For the regular programme this course is taken in the third year of study, and for students on the ASPECT programme it is taken in the fourth year. Students who have taken more years to get to this point will have failed a number of courses at some point so that they were not able to carry these alongside a full load of courses in the following year. The next column in the table shows how many years after taking this third-year course the student graduated. For all students the regular time to do this would be one year. More than one year indicates that either third-year or final-year courses were failed and needed to be repeated. The final column in the table adds together these two numbers to obtain the total years to graduate. For the regular programme this number is four; the ASPECT programme takes five years. Those students who completed in regular time are marked with an asterisk in this column.

Thus it can be seen that only six of these 14 students completed within regular time, in fact a slightly higher proportion than that typically recorded for graduates in this programme (Case 2012). A particular shock emerges in the news that Sizwe failed a number of third-year courses during the year in which he had been

Table 13.1 Academic record of all students in the case study

	ASPECT	Years in programme till 3rd year	Further years to graduate	Total time in the programme (years)
Sizwe	ASPECT	4	2	6
Phumzile	ASPECT	5	1	6
Susan		3	1	4*
Cyril		5	1	6
Rajesh		6	2	8
Sibongile	ASPECT	4	1	5*
Peter		3	1	4*
Andrew		3	2	5
John		3	1	4*
Nkosazana	ASPECT	4	1	5*
Mcebisi	ASPECT	5	2	7
Tshepo	ASPECT	5	1	6
Zanele	ASPECT	4	1	5*
Mpho	ASPECT	4	4	8

Notes

ASPECT is the extended degree programme that spreads the first two years over three years, with supplemental input designed to assist students from disadvantaged school backgrounds

* Indicates students who completed in regulation time for their programme

interviewed, and had not been allowed to proceed to final year in the following year. Here was a student who was charting a laudable path of maintaining a broader set of objectives for his time at university alongside his chemical engineering studies. Yet the structural demands of the programme scuppered his plans. His story continues to give us pause for reflection.

With regard to the rest of Sizwe's classmates, as has been noted earlier, at the time of the study, which took place in a third-year course, a number of these students had already taken extra years to get to that point. Cyril and Rajesh had started in the regular programme, but had repeated two and three years respectively. Of the ASPECT students, Phumzile, Mcebisi and Tshepo had fallen one year behind their entry cohorts. In the narratives all of these students had spoken about the experience of failure, as well as the challenges of reintegrating into a 'new' class.

For advanced reactor engineering, the particular course under review, it has already been noted that two of these 14 students failed the course, namely Cyril and Mpho. It was also noted that in this respect the performance of this group of 14 students was on average better than the overall class, who experienced a pass rate of only 62 per cent.

Despite their relative success at this point, only about two-thirds of this group managed to graduate in the following year. Although he had to repeat the advanced reactor engineering course, Cyril was able to carry this one course alongside the second semester of his final year and graduated successfully at the end of that year. On the other hand, although they had passed this particular course, Sizwe, Andrew and Mcebisi failed a number of other third-year courses, and together with Mpho they only progressed to final year a year later. Rajesh took extra time to graduation because of having to repeat the final-year design project course; Mpho repeated this course twice.

In terms of the overall cohort, of course we also need to note that these were all students who had 'made it' to the third-year course under investigation. In this programme approximately one-third of the entry cohort will already have left the programme, most having been academically excluded. The participants in the study were all students present in the lecture where the invitation to participate was made. The 14 students presented in this book were all those whom it was quite straightforward to track down after graduation. Thus, what is presented here is a perspective from the more successful students in class. And thus, the picture that has been painted so far of the student experience in the programme should give cause for concern. We also need to be reminded that this is a high-status programme at one of the highest-status universities on the African continent. The students recruited to this programme are right at the top of their cohort of school leavers. They have been shown to largely apply themselves with great persistence and dedication to their studies. Yet, for the majority of graduates, ultimate success in this programme involves a lot of failure along the way and repeated years. We have noted here the social difficulties of reintegrating into a new class, but we also need to note the added cost of extra student fees and the lost years of employment.

Some ten years on from the third-year course, it was thus very interesting to catch up with these graduates. All of them were working, with all of them except Susan and Cyril working as process (chemical) engineers. Susan had gone into management consulting after graduation and thereafter into human resource management, and Cyril had spent two years working towards an MSc in chemical engineering and thereafter become a school science teacher. Of those working as process engineers, some were in the production/operations environment (Sibongile, Mcebisi, Mpho), some worked on particular projects within a production company (Peter, Nkosazana) and a number worked for consulting companies doing design work (Rajesh, John and Andrew). In terms of industry, Sizwe, Rajesh, Sibongile, Mcebisi, Nkosazana and Zanele were all working in mining and minerals processing, most of them (all except Mcebisi and Rajesh) having held bursaries from mining companies. Tshepo had gone from mining into the nuclear industry. Phumzile was in the petrochemicals industry, Peter was in paper production, Mpho worked in the chemicals industry, and Andrew and John worked at the same consulting company, which specialised in water treatment. All graduates except Rajesh (who was not a South African citizen and who would have therefore struggled to be eligible for a work visa with his undergraduate engineering degree) were working in South Africa.

Sizwe and Nkosazana were still working for the company that had sponsored both of these students through their studies. Sizwe had not lost his passion for community development; at this stage he was heavily involved in mentoring younger engineers at work, but also giving frequent talks to young people in the community. And he said that in the longer term he still wanted to move out of the corporate world and get into a full-time focus on community development work. Mpho and Zanele were also both in the same company since graduation. All other graduates had had more than one employer since graduation, although both Andrew and Peter, who had done casual work overseas before returning to South Africa, were in the same company where they had started their chemical engineering careers.

A number of students had completed master's degrees at this point, most of which had been sponsored by their employers: Sibongile and Nkosazana had done a master's in innovation and were both following this up with MBAs; John, Andrew and Peter had completed chemical engineering-related master's degrees; Susan was completing a master's in human resource management. Cyril had left his master's studies before submitting his thesis, having struggled again to balance his studies against his family demands. At this point he felt he needed a decisive break both from his immediate family and from his studies – he decided that what he really wanted to do was school teaching.

Most graduates talked about their future plans involving moving on in the fairly short term from their current employers. Sibongile and Mcebisi, who were in the production environment, both stated that one could not do this for too many years more – very demanding hours – and both planned to move onto something else in due course. Sibongile was interested in starting her own business, and Mcebisi said he wanted to go into school teaching since he saw a desperate need there. Others spoke about the need for a new challenge: Peter said after five years in the same company that he was 'feeling like I'm getting to the point where I'm doing a lot of the same thing again and again'. He did not want to be limited to experience in only one industry. Susan said she had learnt that she got bored after a while in the same kind of job, and was relishing the learning curve of a whole new career in HR. Rajesh said the inevitable project-related funding of design work meant that he was always chasing engineering jobs, and felt this was typically the case for most engineers in the context of the high-income country where he worked, which he contrasted to the situation in his home country and in South Africa.

In reflecting back on their undergraduate experience, very few graduates were able to summon up very detailed memories. Most remembered the intensity and were largely relieved that it was over: 'I'm still grateful to have survived,' said Nkosazana. Susan was somewhat unusual in remembering and sharing considerable detail; she still thinks that third-year chemical engineering was her 'worst year ever' in her life. She remembers closely what the design project was like and how lost she had felt. She described third year as being a year with 'no wriggle room', particularly because failing subjects would mean not progressing to final year.

Mcebisi still smarted at what he described as 'unnecessary' years of repeating subjects owing to fickle assessment experiences. Tshepo, on the other hand, felt that his experiences of repeating courses had shaped him into the person that he was, saying 'That's when life developed a meaning for me' – at least partly because he then had a bit more time to enjoy student life. He also felt it had given him a 'thick skin', which had been crucial in the real world. Cyril felt similarly that he had been formed by the struggle of making it through the chemical engineering curriculum. Mpho also said: 'I think I wouldn't have been where I am if some things didn't go wrong in my life.'

Of her time, moving straight through the programme with no repeat years, Sibongile recalled: 'I didn't have much of a life; I could have had more friends.' John, on the other hand, remembered third year as the year when he had really started to enjoy chemical engineering; when it had started to relate to the career that he anticipated.

With regard to how they had used the knowledge from the chemical engineering degree, most of them pointed to the core introductory second-year course on mass and energy balances, and some of them used aspects of final year, for example, finance and process optimisation. The only person who said they used anything from the third-year courses was Tshepo, and he pointed to having learnt how to model a process scientifically, using analytical equations and computer models, rather than the particular content of these courses. Sibongile and Peter both said that they wished they had been able to see the practical application of chemical engineering at the time. Most of them spoke about the significance of the skills that they had obtained in the workplace in informing what they currently did. However, in more general terms, many of them stressed the general value of the degree, for example, Mcebisi, who said: 'Chem eng taught me to think logically.' Nkosazana said: 'Chem eng has shaped my way of thinking – you are taught to think systematically. It's more important sometimes than the actual technical knowledge.' Cyril felt that what he had obtained from the degree was a keen problem-solving skill and the ability to do critical thinking, both of which had been hugely valuable in his teaching career so far.

A couple of them spoke explicitly about the external value of the degree; what Susan described as a 'badge of honour'. Nkosazana said 'people are willing to listen to you – because you studied chem eng'. Tshepo was adamant around this value of the degree:

> The key for UCT engineering [is that] it's not made easy to pass. It separates . . . We boast about being UCT graduates. It shows in industry.

Many of these graduates described the value of the undergraduate experience in terms of being able to cope with anything that came their way. For some this related to their ability to learn new things. Nkosazana said: 'When I get something new now, it's easy to grasp.' Peter related this to having the confidence to tackle new things:

> The degree does prepare you to be confident to tackle new problems. . . . Very often I am tackling new things, you don't know where to start, it's all

new, but you have the confidence to do it. The degree gives you a belief in your ability.

Other students also spoke about their confidence. Andrew said he left final year feeling very confident. Sibongile said: 'Because I did well in the degree, when I got to work, I knew I would do well.' Mpho said the following:

> It makes you a better person, you can make clearer decisions quicker than the average person can do. . . . Some of us came from disadvantaged schools, we were not exposed to a lot of things, even the pressure was good. Even now, if the line is down, you need to make a plan.

In a similar vein, Zanele said the following:

> At UCT you learn to be independent and committed. When you get to work you must be independent and committed, you must love what you do.

For many students 'coping with anything' referred to being able to work under pressure and complete tasks to deadline. Rajesh said:

> Having done that, though, you can handle anything that comes your way. . . . I think anyone who comes out of UCT with engineering, will be a winner. We are pressurised to an extent, you don't see that pressure in the workplace.

Mcebisi said:

> You can give me anything at any time, I can handle it. I don't flinch. I just say 'bring it', I have been through hell before.

Now that we have completed the narratives of the 14 students whose experiences formed the empirical focus for this book, we can turn to the task of building a social realist analysis, first for the immediate context of UCT chemical engineering, and then broadening into a more general consideration of student learning in higher education.

Drawing together the social realist analysis

At the outset of this case study the context for the study was outlined: the chemical engineering programme at the University of Cape Town. There it was seen that an ongoing concern in this programme has been the relatively low success rate of undergraduate students, even though these were selected from some of the very top school achievers in South Africa and further afield. Racially disaggregated, these data have given particular cause for concern, especially in the post-apartheid context, which has a desire for further equity for individuals and development across society. In realist terms this is the level of the 'actual', objectively observed events.

In the case study presented we have explored student narratives as they moved through this programme, from choice of study through a range of dimensions of their experiences of studying. In the preceding section of this chapter we have just completed the narratives all the way through to their careers after graduation. This is the level of the 'empirical', the subjective perceptions of the individual. Although we noted some respects in which a common shared experience could be identified, throughout the narratives the distinctive nature of the individual with their own particular background and their particular capacities was evident. We are now in a position to start to develop a full realist analysis in which we related events at these two levels to the mechanisms at the level of the 'real' by which they are produced. This section thus works towards a perspective on student learning in UCT chemical engineering, which moves up and down all the ontological levels.

We saw that the decision to study chemical engineering at UCT emerges in the context of individuals who are starting to craft a life course. For many students, this decision sets them apart from the typical routes post-schooling in the communities in which they have grown up, and there is thus a need to be in a position to exercise autonomous reflexivity to make such a decision. This involves a process of coming to a self-driven notion of what one wants to do. Autonomous reflexivity will turn out to be a centrally important capacity for success in the programme, and thus we can see one respect in which widening participation to a broader community can involve bringing in students who have strong potential.

It is only those who are achieving good school results in mathematics and physical science who are in a position to even consider engineering. What the narratives illustrate is that, at least for many students, engineering does not come in as a first choice. For many students, especially female students, it appears, engineering is what is left when a number of other professional options have been rejected. It works in the abstract as a route towards doing something significant with one's life, often conceptualised in terms of a better life, either for one's family or for the broader community. South Africa's context of being a middle-income country is very significant in the context of the choice to study engineering. In a context where university fees are not insubstantial for the middle class, and completely unaffordable for the working class, engineering bursaries offer a way forward. Furthermore, with the strong resource base in the economy, chemical engineers are in demand. Structurally these material issues exercise a key role in conditioning the space in which someone chooses chemical engineering.

The nascent 'projects' that are illustrated through narratives of choice need to be reworked as students enter the reality of studying engineering. Here the structural constraints are significant, as manifest in the curriculum and its outworkings in pedagogy. Students find themselves in situational logics that appear to demand exclusive focus on one project, that of meeting academic course demands. The pacing is tight, and even the students who have the strongest academic backgrounds are struggling to fit it all in. The logical message of the curriculum for many is that there is 'no time to think'. For many students coping precludes a decent engagement with the course material.

How can we make sense of this situation in a realist sense? We note the inherent structural constraints of the disciplinary knowledge in the curriculum, that, derived from a hierarchical knowledge structure, is going to make demands for cumulative learning. But we also know that the curriculum is a selection and recontextualisation that reflects an ideological struggle. Here it may not seem an accident that those people who have succeeded in this tight contest (academics) support the continuation of a curriculum structure that tends to exclude all except the very able students. And indeed, successful graduates go on to say that having succeeded in chemical engineering at UCT, they feel they have the confidence to tackle any challenge at hand. Furthermore, the constraints at play mean that only a minority of chemical engineering students manage to include any significant broader development into their time at university. Again, we should not see this as a historical accident. The curriculum is a crafting of the constraints at hand for a particular project of student learning, and the chemical engineering curriculum at UCT, not dissimilar to engineering curricula worldwide, operates towards particular outcomes. The students who manage to 'survive' this challenging curriculum emerge as graduates who are able to work with a large volume of technical material and process it in an efficient manner. These are characteristics that are valued by industry, and thus these graduates have good employment prospects.

At the heart of the academic project in chemical engineering is the individual student who has to acquire and demonstrate a newly specialised consciousness. However, the means to get there, for the vast majority of people, rests hugely on interaction with others. Here again we can note structural and cultural constraints. Emerging from a race- and class-stratified society, we note that for most students the possibilities of networking widely across the class are limited. Students who manage to 'stay on track' in the programme are often bound into close small friendship groups that offer lots of academic support to each other. Students who find themselves stranded without a 'group' are at a distinct disadvantage.

Interaction with the lecturer emerges in this study as a key enabler of student learning. Given the inherent power dynamics of this relationship, it is observed that the lecturer has significant power to craft the social dynamics in ways to either facilitate learning or to allow hindrances to go unchecked. Without significant interaction, and indeed crafting of their role as a true social actor, the accessibility of the lecturer will tend to be differentially experienced depending on a student's primary agency – the demographic markers of their social origins.

Here, then, is the view on student learning in chemical engineering at UCT that starts to emerge in a social realist analysis:

- Curriculum and pedagogy are manifestations of the structural and cultural constraints for student learning, and work both to constrain and enable student learning.
- Students enter this context with highly differentiated personal properties and powers that have been developed in prior educational and other experiences.

- Succeeding in chemical engineering involves meeting an extraordinary set of course demands. The logic of this situation constrains the possibilities for a student to engage in building the kind of conceptual understanding that will be needed for long-term success.
- A small minority of students do succeed in this straitened programme, and an even smaller proportion manage to build in any kind of broader development.
- Academic peer support is a key enabler of student success, as are interactions with the lecturers. These interactions are all conditioned by broader social dynamics. The lecturer has a particular potential to craft new situational logics with regard to student access to support.

Reflecting on the analysis

The realist analysis shows that none of the observed outcomes at UCT chemical engineering can be considered a matter of historical accident. A highly sophisticated system has evolved that has particular outcomes: those students who do graduate, even those who take much more than the regular time to achieve this end, go on to have successful engineering careers in South Africa and abroad. They seem to overcome whatever might have been the limitations of a university experience that did not allow for much more than intense academic focus on chemical engineering and, for many, significant experience of failure. In this latter point we note the costs of such a system. What does it mean for the individual who ends up taking eight years over a four-year degree? A significant proportion of students also spend years in the programme and never graduate, at massive costs to themselves (largely empirically unexplored in this study) and to society. What does it mean for a South African university to note that these experiences remain highly associated with race?

The cost of any significant improvement in student success in the programme will mean that the reputation of its graduates, which derives at least in part from their having 'survived' this programme (in a context where many who enter do not), would need to find another base. Graduates themselves say that they can face anything with confidence, having succeeded in this programme. Thus, a change in the overall success for students in this programme would involve a significant cultural change for all. Can the programme change to achieve better outcomes for more students, and still retain its strong reputation?

Thus, at this relatively simplistic level, we recognise the structural constraints on students achieving success in this programme. Knowledge, with its own causal powers and properties, is central to the academic endeavour. Student success has to be a measure of a student's ability to produce 'legitimate text' in a given academic space. What is legitimate is determined by the academics who run the programme. UCT chemical engineering, as seen here, enacts a particular definition of 'legitimate', and the majority of students do not manage to reach this point within the regular curriculum.

Culturally, the very success of its current graduates has to be an enormous constraint on implementing real change in the system. The situational logics are robust, and neither the interests of the academy or industry would like to see any real challenge to the guarantee that the UCT chemical engineering graduate is one of a small group of survivors of an exceptionally rigorous programme. That white students tend to succeed differentially in this programme is at the end of the day just an inconvenient truth for many.

A simplistic assessment of the situation at hand would suggest something like the following: the programme is failing the majority of its students, thus either it should be made easier or more time should be allocated to allow students to master the necessary work. There are a number of problems with this position, not least of which that it takes the current outcomes of the programme for granted. Fundamentally it plays into credentialism, which sees the value of the degree in instrumental terms focused on a piece of paper.

Working from the normative position established at the outset of this book, which argues for the significance of higher education for building a more socially and environmentally just society, and the special role of professionals in building that society, we need to take a number of steps backwards.

Significantly, we need to consider what is at the heart of our analysis, which is the morphogenesis of student agency. We note that the scope for student growth and action in this programme is extremely limited. The curriculum specifies a close-ended engagement with knowledge, and students need to stick closely to a specified series of course tasks and demands if they are to succeed. Crucially, when graduates are out in the workplace, the significance of the degree is asserted in terms that it gave them the confidence to face anything. Mostly they state that they do not use the knowledge beyond the second year of the programme. They come across as highly self-actualised professionals, but they are not able to point to the value of the advanced knowledge in the programme or their engagement with it. They are mainly able to state that they survived. There is no doubt that this group are individually playing effective roles in society, but the role of the undergraduate programme in their development seems limited to learning to work hard and to survive. It has been a very effective filter.

Thus it is worth asking whether we can envision a programme with a significantly *enlarged* space for the morphogenesis of student agency. If the programme is to do more than simply sift out those students who have the resources to cope with rapid work demands, then it needs to take on a role of allowing students, through a deep engagement with knowledge, to develop into the kind of professionals that are needed in the twenty-first century.

The poor success rates in this programme and in others elsewhere need to be seen as symptoms of a deeper problem, not as the problem in themselves. This is the value of a realist analysis.

Building an undergraduate experience that will allow for true agential morphogenesis will require relatively significant structural and cultural change. It would involve moving away from a model of 'survival of the fittest' towards an assumption that most students who are selected for the programme are expected to succeed, and that they will do so through an intense engagement with themselves, others and with disciplinary knowledge. The structural constraints of knowledge mean that this will continue to be a demanding programme, but it will be demanding in quite a different way. Rather than jumping through highly specified hoops and hurdles, well suited to the thoroughbreds, it will require a changing of oneself and a building of radically new perspectives on the world.

Practically, what would such a curriculum that supported this kind of student learning look like? First, clearly it would need to make sure that it is up to date with contemporary engineering work and future challenges. In this regard, the work of Grasso and Martinelli (2009) seems to signal an important new direction, with their call for a more 'holistic' engineering education. This also links to Sullivan's conceptualisation of what professionalism needs to encompass in the twenty-first century (Sullivan 2004; Sullivan 2011). At the same time, recognising the enormous power of the modern basis of engineering science, curricula need to be structured to support cumulative learning of the fundamentals. A particular challenge for engineering curricula is about how to structure the staged development of students' ability to tackle progressively more open-ended (weakly classified) problems.

Second, we need to realise that there will need to be some change to curriculum content. The current engineering curriculum with its tight pacing and high volume of content militates against good student learning. At the same time as the curriculum is being scrutinised for its relevance, there is going to need to be some chopping of traditional content – especially if space is to be found for new content, as well as more time on open-ended problem-solving. The curriculum needs to develop a new basis for legitimation. It can no longer simply be that it is an assurance that the graduate, as one of the few survivors, can plough through lots of complex work in a short period of time. It also needs to deliver graduates with a particular perspective on the world. It needs to create an environment that demands high levels of engagement based on intrinsic relevance of material, not merely on projected future earnings and the risk of being a failure.

Third, this study has poignantly shown up the reality of the so-called 'flexible' curriculum, where students end up with a cohort other than the one with which they started, either owing to an extended degree programme, or failing courses, or both. There is an enormous benefit to having a curriculum structure where the majority of students progress through it in the same cohort. This is not just a 'nice to have'; it has been shown here that having access to an ongoing peer support group has a central impact on student learning outcomes. In this regard, creative thinking that takes account of the limited resources of most public universities is needed. There is, however, tremendous scope for creative design that uses, for example, the large number of vacation weeks that students have at hand. For example, teaching at UCT happens over a mere 120 days in the year. Current pilot schemes are underway to allow chemical engineering students to do a 'Boot Camp' facilitated by a senior postgraduate, which allows them to work towards a re-examination in a particular course. Early indications are that this has significant potential for supporting student progression and building cumulative understanding. Other institutions will need to explore practical solutions that work in their context.

To bring into effect this curriculum, which offers strong fundamentals, more open-ended and up-to-date engagement, and a sensible pacing of material with support for student progression in a cohort, will require considerable effort from university engineering educators. This is a particular challenge because the current context of the university is one where the sensible response to the situational logics is to expend a minimum of effort on one's teaching. To put your time into curriculum development work is simply insane. If university reward mechanisms do not properly recognise teaching and teaching development work, then none of this change will be possible.

In summary

In this section of the book we have worked through a case study of student learning with a social realist approach. Using narratives of third-year chemical engineering students at the University of Cape Town, we have developed a realist perspective on this situation, which maps out the way in which this system operates to produce particular outcomes. We note the extraordinary achievement of these graduates, which is to learn to cope with a large volume of conceptually difficult work. We also note that this also means that many students struggle to engage deeply with the knowledge at hand, and that overall there are many who do not succeed to progress within the programme as structured. None of this is random; from a realist perspective we have been asking the question of what mechanisms must be operating for the system to give the observed outcomes we note. But the realist analysis also now gives us the parameters within which we can consider alternatives. Specifically, we can start to ask whether it might not be desirable for the programme to foster a broader form of agential morphogenesis, rather than just the narrow straitjacket of tight curriculum demands. The realist analysis also shows that these are not trivial questions: we can see that a lot of current reputational success of the programmes rests precisely on this curriculum structure and on the fact that not all students succeed. Would it be possible to create a programme that keeps the same intensity of engagement but allows for a deeper and more critical engagement with knowledge and thus allows for an enlarged space for graduate agency? These will be explorations going forward.

At this stage in the book, then, we move out from the specific context of UCT chemical engineering and we start to consider the implications of a social realist approach for researching student learning in higher education. We will return to the key questions posed at the outset of this book, which revolve around the morphogenesis of student agency and how we might characterise desirable outcomes for higher education, as well as the morphogenesis of culture and structure that might support such agential change.

Part IV

Drawing the strands together

This book began with an argument that much contemporary education research is limited in its potential impact and that a social realist approach has much to offer in terms of building powerful outputs. Here the focus is on building explanatory theory, working at the level of the real and identifying mechanisms and their emergent causal effects in conditioning the possibilities for student learning. These explanations help us to understand why we have the outcomes we do, and to examine the possibilities for designing systems that might have different outcomes.

A key contribution of Archer's social realist theory is a stratified model of human agency: here we can see that personal identity and social identity are distinct entities, but in tracking their interplay we can note the possibilities for full agential morphogenesis in the student: the emergence of the social actor, who is able to invest him or herself in a social role that expresses what they care about in the world. At this point, any explanation that does not account for the real nature of knowledge, with its own particular properties and powers, will be limited. The development of student agency in higher education is centred on an engagement with knowledge. It has been noted so far that such space for the development of student agency was relatively limited in the programme under scrutiny. If we want to change the possibilities for agential morphogenesis in our undergraduate programmes, then we are really asking about the possibilities for structural and cultural change in the university.

This final part of the book thus brings together the various strands of the argument presented so far and works towards pulling together the key aspects of a social realist analysis of student learning in higher education.

Chapter 14

A social realist approach to research on student learning

A social realist analysis focuses on identifying systems of mechanisms that give rise to observed social phenomena. This is the core focus of the analysis, and in this book is employed towards developing an understanding of the possibilities for change in higher education. One of the distinctive aspects of adopting Archer's specific version of social realist theory is the full characterisation of the agent in terms of their personal properties and powers. Three significant personal properties and powers are identified by Archer: self-consciousness, reflexivity and knowledge. In the context of research on student learning, this involves a different characterisation of students from what has been common across much of the research literature.

The previous section drew together the analysis of student narratives from the chemical engineering programme at the University of Cape Town. It was argued that the current space for the morphogenesis of student agency is limited, and what might be desirable is an enlarging of that space. At this point we build on the general lines of thinking that were developed through that analysis in order to offer a more general analytical perspective on student learning in higher education that is informed by critical realism.

Social realist explanations

At the outset it is important to restate what counts as an explanation in social realism terms. A correlation is not an explanation, and neither is a description. We have many of these in the existing corpus of higher education research. It is not that the data here are not potentially meaningful, but we need to go beyond quantitative correlation and interpretive description in order to build social realist findings. Crucially, we need to ask: how must the world be – in terms of underlying generative mechanisms – for our observations in the actual and empirical to make sense? This outline of a joined-up set of links of emergent causality is what we need to aim for.

Social mechanisms at the level of the real can be characterised in terms of the relations between structure and culture. For a given social setting, for example, a particular course context, we need to trace the prior morphogenetic cycles of structural and cultural elaboration in order to understand the contemporary conditioning that will be in effect. These are the conditions that will both enable and constrain human action. In the case study presented earlier, this involved an unpacking both of the institutional but also of the disciplinary context.

At the heart of the social world is human interaction. This will be the context in which agency is either developed or stilted. We already know from contemporary work in educational theory that the social context for learning is significant. In recent decades we have had work that has emphasised the role of peer interactions; at the same time there has been a misconception that asserts that the role of the teacher is not so important. The case study presented earlier affirms that indeed the teacher has a key role to play in fostering student development.

A social realist perspective on student learning in higher education allows us to think critically about the outcomes of our education systems. Nothing is accidental; education systems are carefully structured and strongly immersed in a cultural space. Once we understand the causal links that explain why we see what we do, then we can start to realistically assess the potentials for change.

Morphogenesis of student agency

Archer's theory offers a rich and nuanced take on agency, and as such makes a distinct contribution to the characterisation of the student experience of learning in higher education. Within her stratified model of human agency, of particular significance is personal identity, which starts to build during childhood and adolescence on a continuous sense of self. The student's choice to pursue a particular course of study can be characterised as resulting from an internal conversation in which the student weighs up their concerns in each of the natural, practical and social orders, then, using emotional commentaries (not only rational deliberations), decides on priorities and formulates a 'project'. The modes in which these international conversations get carried out are encapsulated in the notion of reflexivity. Students using communicative modes of reflexivity tend to externalise their internal conversations and seek approval from their immediate social context for a course of action. The choice to study higher education, for a student who comes from a background where this is not a common option, will thus require another mode of reflexivity: that of autonomous reflexivity in which the student is able to detach from that context and independently formulate a project, usually focused towards achieving competence in the practical domain. A small number of students at this age might engage in meta-reflexivity in which concerns about improving the lot of others are strong drivers for their choices.

At the heart of Archer's morphogenetic cycle is human interaction. In the context of student learning in higher education we note the significance of the development of corporate agency, in which students assist each other towards achieving their goals. The possibilities for engaging in corporate agency can be socially constrained by the peer network possibilities in the class. The interaction between the student and the lecturer appears to be absolutely central to student learning and a key feature of this distinct social context. Here, the lecturer as the more knowledgeable other, who also has the power to judge student performance as adequate or not, is in a strong position to assist students (or not) in mediating the challenges of the curriculum. Here we have characterised as a social actor a lecturer who personifies the role in such a way that they are able to fully enable student learning in their disciplinary area. A social realist perspective asserts that knowledge is real, and as such that it has causal powers. To take on an idea is to put yourself in a particular configuration of situational logics that both constrains and enables your future actions. This is the sense in which realism recognises the causal powers of knowledge. Student learning in higher education is centred on the acquisition of knowledge; the morphogenesis of student agency is defined by knowledge.

Archer's full model for the morphogenesis of human agency is central to this analysis. Here we see the way in which personal and social identity come together. Temporally prior to interaction is the primary agent, the person who is born into a set of life collectivities, what Archer terms the 'conditioned "me"'. In the phase of human interaction we see the development of corporate agency, the 'interactive "we"'. The full outcome of agential morphogenesis is the synthesis of personal identity and social identity into the 'elaborated "you"'. Thus, this should be the end goal of any true higher education: an individual who has been able to formulate ultimate concerns and enact projects towards that end; also a student who occupies that role in a way that gives expression to their personal identity. This is a full description for what was described in the previous section as an 'enlarged' agency.

At this point we need to step back and reflect on contemporary work that emphasises an 'ontological turn' in higher education. Ronald Barnett, building on his earlier work, which characterised curriculum goals in terms of 'knowing', 'acting' and 'being' over the familiar duo of knowledge/skills, in his recent book (Barnett 2007) has suggested that the development of 'being' in higher education has been significantly neglected and requires attention. He characterises 'being' predominantly in terms of the students' 'will to learn' and focuses on the extraordinary phenomenon of student persistence in the face of difficulties. Dall'Alba and Barnacle (2007) extend Barnett's work into a full conceptualisation of learning that centres 'being':

> Knowledge remains important, but the focus is no longer knowledge transfer or acquisition. Instead, knowing is understood as created, embodied and enacted. In other words, the question for students would be not only what they know, but also who they are becoming. Rather than treating knowledge as information that can be accumulated within a (disembodied) mind, learning becomes understood as the development of embodied ways of knowing or, in other words, ways-of-being.
>
> (Dall'Alba & Barnacle 2007: 683)

Building on the Archerian analysis developed through this book, it is suggested that these authors are shooting down something of a straw man. Centring knowledge as the focus for higher education does not imply generic skills or a focus on transfer, or indeed some narrow intellectual quest. The view we have developed here on the morphogenesis of student agency sees the engagement with knowledge as quite central to student 'being' and 'becoming'. These are not polar opposites, indeed to privilege 'knowing' over 'being' or 'being' over 'knowing' is to make an ontological move that is not supported by realism. The full characterisation of the human developed here centres on knowledge and reflexivity, which work closely in partnership around the developing personal and social identity.

A useful contribution at this point comes from the work of Maton, who, building on Bernstein's framework and working within a realist framework, has argued for the significance of 'knower structures' alongside 'knowledge structures' (Maton 2007). Maton develops a continuum of knower structures characterised by the strength of the 'social relation' (a parallel to the 'epistemic relation' that describes the strength of classification and framing of the knowledge structures in a Bernsteinian sense). The strength of the 'social relation' is determined by the extent to which the disciplinary area embodies an 'ideal knower', a certain set of dispositions. In the classic sense, building on the 'two cultures' debates of the 1960s, Maton describes the humanities as embodying a strongly classified and framed social relation (and weak epistemic relation) with the 'cultivated gentleman' at its centre, while the sciences liked to portray themselves as a democratic society open to all, regardless of personal disposition. These characterisations of a disciplinary area define its basis for legitimation: 'the means whereby intellectual and educational fields are maintained, reproduced, transformed and changed' (Maton 2007: 93). In considering possible constellations, Maton makes the important point that the strengths of the epistemic and social relation can vary independently of each other. In Barnett's 'ontological turn' and, indeed, in the characterisation of the ideal morphogenesis of student agency depicted in this book, we can thus note a call for the strengthening of the social relation, of a stronger specialisation of knower disposition. Tellingly, Maton characterises a field with both strong social and epistemic relations as an 'elite' code. Herein lies a caution in terms of extra hurdles that we might be suggesting for students who come from a broad range of social backgrounds.

Drawing together then a social realist perspective on student learning in higher education, we can summarise the following key points:

- Curriculum operates as the key manifestation of the structural and cultural conditioning of the space for student learning.
- Student agency needs to be characterised in all its dimensions, defined by past learning experiences, existing as the power to mediate the curriculum and its constraints.
- The central role of human interaction in student learning must be recognised: both peer interaction and even more centrally the interaction with the lecturer.

- The causal powers of knowledge, existing in the domain of the real, at the heart of higher education, need to be asserted.
- Full agential morphogenesis for the student will involve a synthesis of personal identity in concert with a social identity relating to being a student.

As an exemplar, the analysis of student learning in the context of the chemical engineering programme at UCT pointed to some of the shortcomings of that programme. The structural and cultural conditioning of that programme is not some bizarre outlier on the global scale; on the contrary, it derives strongly from its historical engagement with engineering education on the international level. The students who are recruited to this programme are some of the top school leavers in South Africa, together with top students from across the African continent, and thus whatever might be considered the shortcomings of their school education, these again are not entirely unknown issues in other parts of the world. Thus there are aspects of key features of the analysis presented in the previous chapter that will be recognised in other higher education contexts elsewhere.

In looking forward, the detailed analysis presented in this previous chapter pointed to the need for an enlargement of the possibilities for the exercising of student agency in this programme. What is being put forward here is really a revisioning of the goals of that programme as a true *higher* education, and thus a link back to the opening considerations in this book in which the crucial importance of higher education for the building of broad social well-being and environmental sustainability and not just economic development was asserted.

Practically, then, how might we achieve a form of higher education that better accounts for student agency in all its rich layers, and builds a morphogenesis of that agency towards the kinds of graduates who will support the kind of society that has been envisaged?

Possibilities for morphogenesis of structure and culture in higher education

Key aspects of the critical realist perspective include the assertion of a stratified reality, with distinct ontological layers of the actual (objective events), the empirical (subjective experience) and the real (underlying non-observable causal mechanisms). Archer's social realist theory works with two key causal mechanisms at the level of the real: structure and culture. Through a temporal cycle in which the configuration of structure and culture deriving from past events is seen to condition the possibilities for the exercise of human agency in the present, we can analyse over time the events that give rise either to change in social relations (morphogenesis) or a maintenance of the status quo (morphostasis).

A crucial starting point in mapping out a desirable future for student learning in higher education is that universities need to assert their vision for the purposes of higher education more strongly. We have noted how so much of this space has been captured by economic arguments, especially in contemporary times where neo-liberalism means that the state has also tended to cede priority to the economy. The UK sociologist and higher education scholar, Sue Clegg (2008), has noted the relatively meek adoption of these views by the academy, especially at the levels of leadership, and argues for the importance of a reclaiming of that academic space. In terms of a social realist analysis, though, the special role that the academy plays in the realm of culture is significant. In order for morphogenesis of culture to succeed, we need to be prepared to work in a mode that is contradictory to much of contemporary common-sense thinking. Here it is important to note that the current global recession represents a massive shift in the structural arena, which is starting to open up the space for such cultural morphogenesis. We need to remember that this economic repurposing of higher education is a relatively recent phenomenon and thus may be less enduring than might have been feared. However, the structural change of a massified higher education that takes in a large proportion of the school-leaving cohort is an important feature that is unlikely to change, especially in the context of current employment patterns. Thus, it will be important to lever this structural reality in building new arguments about future directions for higher education.

Here, building on opening references to the work of Nussbaum and others, we will thus reassert the significance of higher education, not only as a private investment, or even as a necessity for supplying the skills for a modern economy, but working also within a broader purpose towards the public good. Universities are institutions dedicated towards preserving and extending the stock of knowledge for the future good of humankind. Graduates should be those who have a deep understanding of how knowledge is generated, and are able to critically engage with important issues of the day, in the light of all the resources of the past.

Now we need to shift to a consideration of how to effect the student learning that will be at the heart of the university. No longer the preserve of the elite, we note that students will enter higher education with many different orientations and backgrounds. Using Archer's work, these can be considered more usefully as nascent expressions of personal identity: aspirant students have started to identify what they care about and have formulated personal projects in response to a prioritisation of concerns. Crucially, these decisions are always made on incomplete information and thus are almost implicitly flawed. Moving through university studies will require a frequent reworking on the personal project. Thus we should not dismiss the student who has entered engineering because it was the only route to funding his studies (with an industrial bursary) – we need rather to note that inspiration and growing sophistication of this personal project is an important core to the university experience. Lecturers are uniquely placed to help build this growing identity (a synthesis of the personal and social) through an engagement with knowledge and a projection forward to life after university.

In the context of student learning in higher education, we thus need to begin any analysis with an understanding of the structural and cultural conditioning of the space. A key manifestation of such conditioning in this context is the curriculum. As a structural feature it defines the temporal space wherein students learn.

As culture it sets the boundaries for student engagements with knowledge. Any curriculum emerges from a complex web of past decisions, of struggles for legitimacy within the academy.

Central to the student experience of learning in higher education needs to be a challenging engagement with knowledge. Any educational proposal that seeks to diminish this challenge or to evacuate the centrality of knowledge should be treated with great suspicion. Tamsin Haggis (2006) notes how a focus on 'learner needs' can link to a pathologising of students, a shutting down of potential for the enlargement of student agency, and contrasts this with a focus on intellectual challenge:

> The idea of responding to need suggests that the institution has a responsibility to find out either 'what's wrong' with students, or 'what it is that they want', and to try to provide an appropriate response to this. Challenge, on the other hand, suggests that the institution has something worthwhile to offer; something which may intrinsically, and perhaps even deliberately, incorporate difficulty and struggle.
>
> (Haggis 2006: 531)

Thus, the central task in higher education is building the environment that supports learners in navigating these boundaries and in building specialised knowledge in the discipline. Haggis emphasises the serious limitations of any approach to student learning that sees learning skills as generic and separate from the special requirements of the discipline. Thus we are talking about pedagogical approaches that make explicit to students the discourses and the practices of the discipline. These are not generally self-evident to the student, and why should they be? The whole purpose of higher education is induction into a new way of thinking.

We cannot ignore the developing social identity of students. Moving from primary agency to at least corporate agency is going to be an important shift for many students at the undergraduate level. Peer collaborations can be crucially important in navigating the challenges of higher education. Many students enter higher education to some degree locked in the constraints of the primary agency of their background, with respect to race, class or gender. Higher education is an important space where social identity can develop to build networks that go beyond these constraints.

It can be noted here that undergraduate education is premised on the attainment of autonomous reflexivity. For many students, though, on entry to higher education it might well be communicative reflexivity that is their more dominant mode of decision-making. Once again, in recognising student agency in a fuller sense, we need to note the space for potential shifts in reflexivity and promote that development. Furthermore, in an orientation towards the public good purposes of higher education, it might be desired that at least some engagement with meta-reflexivity, the fashioning of life purposes towards the general good of others, might be a dimension of the undergraduate experience.

At this point we need to take a step back and note the ways in which higher education can operate to limit rather than enlarge the space for the exercise of human agency. In considering this issue, Mann (2007: 131) points to the significant negative impact of 'assessment, especially examinations, overloaded curricula, unrealistic timeframes and impersonal social and institutional relations' on the student, working towards an experience of alienation. She provides a vivid characterisation of a university environment that could work in the opposite direction, towards an opening up of possibilities for the development of agency:

> A culture of learning and inquiry can replace a culture of expertise. In such a culture of learning, making mistakes, taking risks, unpredictability and failure are valued as *necessary* to learning. Lecturers also act as learners, modelling open, cooperative, and relaxed approaches to meaning-making. Dialogue and discussion become central to seeking and clarifying understanding, analysing the significance of material both for itself and for individual students, and for exchanging feedback. Students can be provided with varied opportunities to express and try out their capabilities. Such opportunities include structured, meaningful activities which require cooperative engagement between students who would not normally work together and which provide students with opportunities to investigate and work things out for themselves. Crucially, these activities are given enough time and space for students to feel in control over and responsible for their own learning.
>
> (Mann 2007: 137)

Archer has suggested that the conditions of late modernity involve increased demands on reflexivity. Significantly, within advanced capitalist economies the space for communicative reflexivity is contracting, and the pressures for the exercise of autonomy are increasing. In this latter regard she writes that:

> . . . the new logic of opportunity demands the continuous revision of personal projects, involving the successful monitoring of self, society and relations between them, and denies the establishment of an unchanging *modus vivendi*. In other words, the imperative to be reflexive intensifies with the demise of routine action . . .
>
> (Archer 2007c: 44)

Interestingly too, she considers that the space for meta-reflexivity is also expanding in this context of 'nascent' globalisation. These practitioners she characterises as 'patrons of a new civil society expressive of humanistic values' (Archer 2007c: 44).

Herein we can see a significant – yet often undervalued – value of higher education, in its contribution towards developing a cohort of individuals who are able to not only individually navigate the demands of the evolving new order, but also contribute towards effecting positive change in society.

Bibliography

Archer, M.S. (1995) *Realist social theory: The morphogenetic approach*, Cambridge: Cambridge University Press.

Archer, M.S. (1996) *Culture and agency: The place of culture in social theory*, Cambridge: Cambridge University Press.

Archer, M.S. (2000) *Being human: The problem of agency*, Cambridge: Cambridge University Press.

Archer, M.S. (2003) *Structure, agency and the internal conversation*, Cambridge: Cambridge University Press.

Archer, M.S. (2007a) *Making our way through the world: Human reflexivity and social mobility*, Cambridge: Cambridge University Press.

Archer, M.S. (2007b) 'Realism and the problem of agency', *Journal of Critical Realism*, 5: 11–20.

Archer, M.S. (2007c) 'The trajectory of the morphogenetic approach', *Sociologia, problemas e práticas*, 54: 35–47.

Archer, M.S. (2008) 'For structure: its reality, properties and powers: A reply to Anthony King', *The Sociological Review*, 48: 464–472.

Archer, M.S. (2010) 'Routine, reflexivity, and realism', *Sociological Theory*, 28: 272–303.

Ashwin, P. (2008) 'Accounting for structure and agency in "close-up" research on teaching, learning and assessment in higher education', *International Journal of Educational Research*, 47: 151–158.

Ashwin, P. (2009) *Analysing teaching–learning interactions in higher education: Accounting for structure and agency*, London: Continuum.

ASSAf (2010) *The PhD study: An evidence-based study on how to meet the demands for high-level skills in an emerging economy*, Pretoria: Academy of Sciences of South Africa (ASSAf).

Badat, S. (2009) 'The role of higher education in society: Valuing higher education', paper presented at the HERS-SA Academy 2009, Cape Town, 14 September 2009.

Badat, S. (2011) '13 theses on community engagement in higher education', paper presented at the South African Higher Education Community Engagement Forum Conference, East London, 8 November 2011.

Barnett, R. (2007) *A will to learn: Being a student in an age of uncertainty*, Maidenhead, UK: Society for Research into Higher Education & Open University Press.

Becker, F.S. (2010) 'Why don't young people want to become engineers? Rational reasons for disappointing decisions', *European Journal of Engineering Education*, 35: 349–366.

Becker, H.S., Geer, B. & Hughes, E.C. (1968) *Making the grade: The academic side of college life*, New York: John Wiley and Sons.

Bernstein, B. (1999) 'Vertical and horizontal discourse: An essay', *British Journal of Sociology of Education*, 20: 157–173.

Bernstein, B. (2000) *Pedagogy, symbolic control, and identity: Theory, research, critique*, Lanham, MD: Rowman & Littlefield Publishers.

Bhaskar, R. (1975) *A realist theory of science*, Leeds: Leeds Books.

Bhaskar, R. (1989) *Reclaiming reality: A critical introduction to contemporary philosophy*, London: Verso.

Bhaskar, R. (1998) *The possibility of naturalism: A philosophical critique of the contemporary human sciences*, London: Routledge.

Biggs, J.B. (1978) 'Individual and group differences in study processes', *British Journal of Educational Psychology*, 48: 266–279.

Board on Engineering Education (1995) *Engineering education: Designing an adaptive system*, Washington, DC: National Academy Press.

Boughey, C. (2007) 'Educational development in South Africa: From social reproduction to capitalist expansion?', *Higher Education Policy*, 20: 5–18.

Brown, P., Lauder, H. & Ashton, D. (2011) *The global auction: The broken promises of education, jobs, and incomes*, Oxford: Oxford University Press.

Bruner, J.S. (1985) *Actual minds, possible worlds*, Cambridge, MA: Harvard University Press.

Carter, B. & New, C. (eds) (2004) *Making realism work: Realist social theory and empirical research*, London: Routledge.

Case, J.M. (2007) 'Alienation and engagement: Exploring students' experiences of studying engineering', *Teaching in Higher Education*, 12: 119–133.

Case, J.M. (2012) 'Every generation has its struggle: A critical realist perspective on student learning in contemporary South Africa', Inaugural lecture, University of Cape Town. URL: http://www.youtube.com/watch?v=UrnqrrzQ_HE

Case, J.M. & Gunstone, R.F. (2003) 'Going deeper than deep and surface approaches: A study of students' perceptions of time', *Teaching in Higher Education*, 8: 55–69.

Case, J.M. & Gunstone, R.F. (2006) 'Metacognitive development: A view beyond cognition', *Research in Science Education*, 36: 51–67.

Case, J.M. & Marshall, D. (2004) 'Between deep and surface: Procedural approaches to learning in engineering contexts', *Studies in Higher Education*, 29: 605–615.

Case, J.M. & Marshall, D. (2008) 'The "no problem" Discourse model: Exploring an alternative way of researching student learning', *International Journal of Educational Research*, 47: 200–207.

Case, J.M. & Marshall, D. (2009) 'Approaches to learning', *In:* Tight, M., Huisman, J., Mok, K.H. & Morphew, C. (eds) *The Routledge International Handbook of Higher Education*, London and New York: Routledge Falmer.

Case, J.M., Marshall, D. & Linder, C. (2010) 'Being a student again: A narrative study of a teacher's experience', *Teaching in Higher Education*, 15: 423–433.

Clegg, S. (2008) 'Economic calculation, market incentives and academic identity: Breaking the research/teaching dualism?', *International Journal of Management Concepts and Philosophy*, 3: 19–29.

Collier, A. (ed.) (1998) *Stratified explanation and Marx's conception of history*, London: Routledge.

Collins, R. (2000) *The sociology of philosophies: A global theory of intellectual change*, Cambridge, MA: Harvard University Press.

Cousin, G. (2009) *Researching learning in higher education: An introduction to contemporary methods and approaches*, New York: Routledge.

Crotty, M. (1998) *The foundations of social research: Meaning and perspective in the research process*, Sydney, Australia: Allen & Unwin.

Crouch, C.H. & Mazur, E. (2001) 'Peer instruction: Ten years of experience and results', *American Journal of Physics*, 69: 970–977.

Dall'Alba, G. & Barnacle, R. (2007) 'An ontological turn for higher education', *Studies in Higher Education*, 32: 679–691.

Danermark, B. (2002) *Explaining society: Critical realism in the social sciences*, London: Routledge.

Divall, C. (1994) 'Education for design and production: Professional organization, employers, and the study of chemical engineering in British universities, 1922 1976', *Technology and Culture*, 35: 258–288.

Florida, R. (2005) 'The world is spiky: Globalization has changed the economic playing field but hasn't levelled it', *The Atlantic Monthly*, October.

Flyvbjerg, B. (2001) *Making social science matter*, Cambridge: Cambridge University Press.

Gee, J.P. (2005) *An introduction to discourse analysis: Theory and method*, London: Routledge.

Godfrey, E. & Parker, L. (2010) 'Mapping the cultural landscape in engineering education', *Journal of Engineering Education*, 99: 5–22.

Grasso, D. & Burkins, M.D. (eds) (2009) *Holistic engineering education: Beyond technology*, New York: Springer.

Grasso, D. & Martinelli, D. (2009) 'Holistic engineering', *In:* Grasso, D. & Burkins, M.D. (eds) *Holistic engineering education: Beyond technology*, New York: Springer.

Habib, A. (2012) Dying for a chance at higher education. URL: http://www.uj.ac.za/EN/Newsroom/News/Pages/DyingforachanceathighereducationbyAdamHabib201101162.aspx [15 January 2012].

Hagel, P., Carr, R. & Devlin, M. (2011) 'Conceptualising and measuring student engagement through the Australasian Survey of Student Engagement (AUSSE): A critique', *Assessment & Evaluation in Higher Education*, 1–12.

Haggis, T. (2006) 'Pedagogies for diversity: Retaining critical challenge amidst fears of "dumbing down"', *Studies in Higher Education*, 31: 521–535.

Harré, R., Aronson, J. & Way, E. (1994) *Realism rescued: How scientific progress is possible*, London: Duckworth.

Harwood, J. (2006) 'Engineering education between science and practice: Rethinking the historiography', *History and Technology*, 22: 53–79.

Hill, L.D., Baxen, J., Craig, A.T. & Namakula, H. (2012) 'Citizenship, social justice, and evolving conceptions of access to education in South Africa: Implications for research', *Review of Research in Education*, 36: 239–260.

Hsieh, C. & Knight, L. (2008) 'Problem-based learning for engineering students: An evidence-based comparative study', *The Journal of Academic Librarianship*, 34: 25–30.

Hunter, M. (2010) 'Racial desegregation and schooling in South Africa: Contested geographies of class formation', *Environment and planning*, A, 42: 2640.

Institution of Engineers of Australia (1996) *Changing the culture: Engineering education into the future*, Canberra: IEAust.

Jawitz, J. & Case, J.M. (1998) 'Exploring the reasons given by South African students for studying engineering', *International Journal of Engineering Education*, 14: 235–240.

Jawitz, J., Case, J. & Tshabalala, M. (2000) 'Why NOT engineering? The process of career choice amongst South African female students', *International Journal of Engineering Education*, 16: 470–475.

Johnson, D.W., Johnson, R.T. & Smith, K.A. (1991) *Active learning: Cooperation in the college classroom*, Edina, MN: Interaction Book Company.

Jørgensen, U. (2007) 'Historical accounts of engineering education', *In:* Crawley, E.F., Malmqvist, J., Ostlund, S. & Brodeur, D.R. (eds) *Rethinking engineering education: The CDIO approach*, New York: Springer.

Kahn, P. (2009) 'On establishing a *modus vivendi*: The exercise of agency in decisions to participate or not participate in higher education', *London Review of Education*, 7: 261–270.

King, R. (2008) *Engineers for the future: Addressing the supply and quality of Australian engineering graduates for the 21st century*, Canberra: Australian Council of Engineering Deans.

Kloot, B. (2011) 'A Bourdieuian analysis of foundation programmes within the field of engineering education: Two South African case studies', unpublished PhD thesis, University of Cape Town.

Kotta, L. (2011) 'Structural conditioning and mediation by student agency: A case study of success in chemical engineering design', unpublished PhD thesis, University of Cape Town.

Kuh, G.D. (2003) 'What we're learning about student engagement from NSSE: Benchmarks for effective educational practices', *Change: The Magazine of Higher Learning*, 35: 24–32.

Lave, J. (1996) 'Teaching, as learning, in practice', *Mind, Culture, and Activity*, 3: 149–164.

Leach, J. & Scott, P. (2003) 'Individual and sociocultural views of learning in science education', *Science & Education*, 12: 91–113.

Luckett, K. (2010) 'Knowledge claims and codes of legitimation: Implications for curriculum recontextualisation in South African higher education', *Africanus*, 40: 6–20.

Luckett, K. (2012) 'Working with "necessary contradictions": A social realist meta-analysis of an academic development programme review', *Higher Education Research & Development*, 31: 339–352.

Malcolm, J. & Zukas, M. (2001) 'Bridging pedagogic gaps: Conceptual discontinuities in higher education', *Teaching in Higher Education*, 6: 33–42.

Mann, C.R. (1918) *Report of the Joint Committee on Engineering Education*, Boston, MA: Merrymount Press.

Mann, S.J. (2007) *Study, power and the university*, Milton Keynes: Open University Press.

Marginson, S. (2006) 'Putting "public" back into the public university', *Thesis Eleven*, 84: 44–59.

Marginson, S. (2007) 'University mission and identity for a post post-public era', *Higher Education Research & Development*, 26: 117–131.

Marginson, S. (2008) 'Global field and global imagining: Bourdieu and worldwide higher education', *British Journal of Sociology of Education*, 29: 303–315.

Marginson, S. (2011) 'Higher education in East Asia and Singapore: Rise of the Confucian model', *Higher Education*, 61: 587–611.

Marginson, S. (2012) Online open education: Yes, this is the game changer. *The Conversation*. URL: http://theconversation.edu.au/online-open-education-yes-this-is-the-game-changer-8078

Marshall, D. & Case, J.M. (2010) 'Rethinking "disadvantage" in higher education: A paradigmatic case study using narrative analysis', *Studies in Higher Education*, 35: 491–504.

Marton, F. & Säljö, R. (1976a) 'On qualitative differences in learning: I – Outcome and process', *British Journal of Educational Psychology*, 46: 4–11.

Marton, F. & Säljö, R. (1976b) 'On qualitative differences in learning: II – Outcome as a function of the learner's conception of the task', *British Journal of Educational Psychology*, 46: 115–127.

Maton, K. (2005) 'A question of autonomy: Bourdieu's field approach and higher education policy', *Journal of Education Policy*, 20: 687–704.

Maton, K. (2007) 'Knowledge–knower structures in intellectual and educational fields', *In:* Christie, F. & Martin, J. (eds) *Language, knowledge and pedagogy: Functional linguistic and sociological perspectives*, London: Continuum.

Maton, K. (2009) 'Cumulative and segmented learning: Exploring the role of curriculum structures in knowledge-building', *British Journal of Sociology of Education*, 30: 43–57.

Maton, K. (2010) 'Canons and progress in the arts and humanities: Knowers and gazes', *In:* Moore, R. & Maton, K. (eds) *Social realism, knowledge and the sociology of education: Coalitions of the mind*, London: Continuum.

Mauss, M. (1989) 'A category of the human mind: The notion of person', *In:* Carrithers, M., Collins, S. & Lukes, S. (eds) *The category of the person*, Cambridge: Cambridge University Press.

Mogashana, D., Case, J.M. & Marshall, D. (2012) 'What do student learning inventories really measure? A critical analysis of students' responses to the Approaches to Learning and Studying Inventory', *Studies in Higher Education*, 37: 783–792.

Moore, R. (2009) *Towards the sociology of truth*, London: Continuum.

Moore, R. (2012) 'Social realism and the problem of the problem of knowledge in the sociology of education', *British Journal of Sociology of Education*, 1–21.

Morrow, W.E. (2009) *Bounds of democracy: Epistemological access in higher education*, Cape Town: HSRC Press.

Muller, J. (2000) *Reclaiming knowledge: Social theory, curriculum, and education policy*, London: RoutledgeFalmer.

Muller, J. (2006) 'Differentiation and progression in the curriculum', *In:* Young, M. & Gamble, J. (eds) *Knowledge, curriculum and qualifications for South African further education*, Cape Town: Human Sciences Research Council.

Nakhleh, M.B. (1992) 'Why some students don't learn chemistry: Chemical misconceptions', *Journal of Chemical Education*, 69: 191–196.

National Academy of Engineering (2004) *Educating the engineer of 2020: Adapting engineering education to the new century*, Washington, DC: National Academy Press.

Nixon, J. (2011) *Higher education and the public good*, London: Continuum.

Nixon, R. (1994) *Homelands, Harlem, and Hollywood: South African culture and the world beyond*, New York: Routledge.

Noble, D.F. (1977) *America by design*, New York: Alfred A. Knopf.

Nussbaum, M.C. (2010) *Not for profit: Why democracy needs the humanities*, Princeton, NJ: Princeton University Press.

Park, E.J. & Light, G. (2009) 'Identifying atomic structure as a threshold concept: Student mental models and troublesomeness', *International Journal of Science Education*, 31: 233–258.

Pfundt, H. & Duit, R. (1994) *Bibliography: Students' alternative frameworks and science education*, Kiel: IPN.

Polkinghorne, D. (1995) 'Narrative configuration in qualitative analysis', *In:* Hatch, J.A. & Wisniewski, R. (eds) *Life history and narrative: Influences of feminism and culture*, London: Falmer.

Popper, K. (1966) *Objective knowledge. A realist view of logic, physics and history*, Oxford: Clarendon Press.

Posner, G.J., Strike, K.A., Hewson, P.W. & Gertzog, W.A. (1982) 'Accommodation of a scientific conception: Toward a theory of conceptual change', *Science Education*, 66: 211–227.

Prieto, E., Holbrook, A., Bourke, S., O'Connor, J., Page, A. & Husher, K. (2009) 'Influences on engineering enrolments. A synthesis of the findings of recent reports', *European Journal of Engineering Education*, 34: 183–203.

Ramsden, P. (2003) *Learning to teach in higher education*, London: Routledge.

Rosenthal, J.S. (1995) 'Active learning strategies in advanced mathematics classes', *Studies in Higher Education*, 20: 223–228.

Rowland, S. (1996) 'Relationships between teaching and research', *Teaching in Higher Education*, 1: 7–20.

Sayer, A. (1992) *Method in social science: A realist approach*, Oxford: Routledge.

Sayer, A. (2000) *Realism and social science*, London: Sage.

Sayer, A. (2005) *The moral significance of class*, Cambridge: Cambridge University Press.

Schreuders, P.D., Mannon, S.E. & Rutherford, B. (2009) 'Pipeline or personal preference: Women in engineering', *European Journal of Engineering Education*, 34: 97–112.

Scott, I., Yeld, N. & Hendry, J. (2007) *A case for improving teaching and learning in South African higher education*, Pretoria: Council on Higher Education (CHE) and Higher Education Quality Committee (HEQC).

Sen, A.K. (1999) *Development as freedom*, Oxford: Oxford University Press.

Seymour, E. (1995) 'The loss of women from science, mathematics and engineering undergraduate majors: An explanatory account', *Science Education*, 79: 437–473.

Sfard, A. (1998) 'On two metaphors for learning and the dangers of choosing just one', *Educational Researcher*, March: 4–13.

Sheppard, S. (2009) *Exploring the engineering student experience: Findings from the Academic Pathways of People Learning Engineering Survey (APPLES)*, Center for the Advancement of Engineering Education, TR-10-01.

Shipway, B. (2011) *A critical realist perspective of education*, London: Routledge.

Sjøberg, S., Schreiner, C., Bauer, M., Allum, N. & Shukla, R. (2010) 'The next generation of citizens: Attitudes to science among youngsters', *In:* Bauer, M., Allum, N. & Shukla, R. (eds) *The culture of science: How does the public relate to science across the globe?*, New York: Routledge.

Slaton, A.E. (2010) *Race, rigor, and selectivity in US engineering: The history of an occupational color line*, Cambridge, MA: Harvard University Press.

Smit, R. (2012a) 'Engineering science and pure science: Do disciplinary differences matter in engineering education?', paper presented at the Australasian Association for Engineering Education (AAEE) Annual Conference, Melbourne, 3–5 December 2012.

Smit, R. (2012b) 'Towards a clearer understanding of student disadvantage in higher education: Problematising deficit thinking', *Higher Education Research & Development*, 31: 369–380.

Smith, K.A., Sheppard, S.D., Johnson, D.W. & Johnson, R.T. (2005) 'Pedagogies of engagement: Classroom-based practices', *Journal of Engineering Education*, 94: 87.

Smith, L.C. (2012) 'The effect of selected academic development programmes on the academic performance of academic development students at a South African university: An empirical analysis', unpublished PhD thesis, University of Cape Town.

Snyder, B.R. (1971) *The hidden curriculum*, New York: Alfred A. Knopf.

Spinks, N., Silburn, N. & Birchall, D. (2006) *Educating engineers for the 21st century: The industry view*, London: Royal Academy of Engineering.

Stonyer, H. (2002) 'Making engineering students – Making women: The discursive context of engineering education', *International Journal of Engineering Education*, 18: 392–399.

Sullivan, W.M. (2004) *Work and integrity: The crisis and promise of professionalism in America*, San Francisco, CA: Jossey-Bass.

Sullivan, W.M. (2011) 'Professional education: Aligning knowledge, expertise, and public purpose', *In:* Lagemann, E.C. & Lewis, H. (eds) *What is college for? The public purpose of higher education*, New York: Teachers College Press.

Tate, E.D. & Linn, M.C. (2005) 'How does identity shape the experiences of women of color engineering students?', *Journal of Science Education and Technology*, 14: 483–493.

Tinto, V. (1993) *Leaving college: Rethinking the causes and cures of student departure*, Chicago: University of Chicago Press.

Trow, M. (2006) 'Reflections on the transition from elite to mass to universal access: Forms and phases of higher education in modern societies since WWII', *In:* Forest, J.J.F. & Altbach, P.G. (eds) *International handbook of higher education*, Dordrecht: Springer.

Unterhalter, E. & Carpentier, V. (2010) *Global inequalities and higher education: Whose interests are we serving?*, London: Palgrave Macmillan.

von Blottnitz, H. (2006) 'Promoting active learning in sustainable development: Experiences from a 4th year chemical engineering course', *Journal of Cleaner Production*, 14: 916–923.

Walker, M. (2010) 'A human development and capabilities "prospective analysis" of global higher education policy', *Journal of Education Policy*, 25: 485–501.

Webb, G. (1997) 'Deconstructing deep and surface: Towards a critique of phenomenography', *Higher Education*, 33: 195–212.

Wheelahan, L. (2009) 'The problem with CBT (and why constructivism makes things worse)', *Journal of Education and Work*, 22: 227–242.

Wickstrom, G. & Bendix, T. (2000) 'The "Hawthorne effect": What did the original Hawthorne studies actually show?', *Scandinavian Journal of Work, Environment & Health*, 26: 363–367.

Williams, K.F. (2012) 'Rethinking "learning" in higher education: Viewing the student as social actor', *Journal of Critical Realism*, 11: 296–323.

Wolmarans, N., Luckett, K. & Case, J.M. (2012) 'Investigating principles of curriculum knowledge progression: A case study of design in a civil engineering degree programme', paper presented at the Seventh International Basil Bernstein Symposium, Aix-en-Provence.

Young, M. (2008) *Bringing knowledge back in: From social constructivism to social realism in the sociology of education*, London: RoutledgeFalmer.

Young, M. & Muller, J. (2010) 'Three educational scenarios for the future: Lessons from the sociology of knowledge', *European Journal of Education*, 45: 11–27.

Index